D1049661

"Let your Kingdom come"

For centuries lovers of God and of righteousness have been praying, "Let your kingdom come." World events in fulfillment of Bible prophecy prove that God's kingdom is now at hand. It is hoped that this book will help you to reach out for a share in the grand blessings that the Kingdom will provide for mankind right here on our earth.

—The Publishers

Publishers
WATCHTOWER BIBLE AND TRACT SOCIETY
OF NEW YORK, INC.
INTERNATIONAL BIBLE STUDENTS ASSOCIATION
BROOKLYN, NEW YORK, U.S.A.

This Book Is Published in 29 Languages
Total Books Printed of All Editions
14,000,000 COPIES

Made in the United States of America

"LET YOUR KINGDOM COME"

CONTENTS

NOTE: Bible quotations in this book are from the modern-language *New World Translation of the Holy Scriptures.*

In connection with dates, the abbreviation B.C.E. means "Before the Common Era," and C.E. means "Of the Common Era."

CHAPTER 1

"THY KINGDOM COME"!

FEW WORDS of prayer have been repeated more often than the above. Perhaps you the reader have uttered that prayer. And surely we need God's kingdom! How grand it would be to live under the conditions pictured on these pages! And that is the hope that God's kingdom

Questions for Discussion: 1. What would God's kingdom mean to you, if soon it brought the conditions pictured here?

holds out for us: Peace and harmony in all the earth. The races of mankind united in bonds of genuine love. Everyone delighting to do productive work and enjoying the fruits of his labors. The air filled with the music of creation and with the song and laughter of happy humans. A healthy global society of mankind in which no one grows old or gets sick. The enjoyment of peace with the animals, the fragrance of flowers, the beauty of colorful landscapes and ever-changing seasons. Yes, all of this, and much more, is promised for our earth after God's kingdom comes, as we shall see.

[2] However, things are far different now. For we are passing through times that the Bible describes as "hard to deal with." (2 Timothy 3:1) You know how these critical times have touched your own life. Many who will read these pages have lost loved ones in the wars and other violence of this century. Yet the nations are engaged in the most feverish armaments race of all time. And they already have on hand far more than enough weapons to bring about the annihilation of all humankind.

[3] Other problems, very close to home, also concern us. With the upsurge of muggings, murder and rape, many of us find it dangerous even to walk the streets. And do we not hear of more divorces, broken families and delinquency than formerly? In this age of permissive sex and drug addiction, many persons are apprehensive about sending their children to the public schools. If you live in some neighborhood or country where such problems have not yet surfaced, you should be thankful indeed!

2, 3. What changes in recent years emphasize the need for God's kingdom?

[4] How much does it cost to put food on your table these days? And how much does it cost to run your automobile? As food and fuel prices soar, the shaky world situation casts ominous shadows into the future. Where is our world headed? An item in *U.S. News & World Report* of August 4, 1980, underlined the seriousness of the crisis. It said: "Unless major new steps are taken, the world 20 years from now will be a filthy, unstable planet with billions of poor people scrambling for scarce, high-priced resources. That warning emerged on July 24 from a presidential commission completing a three-year study." Among other things, this study revealed that by the year 2000 the world's population will reach 6.3 billion, that—inflation aside—food prices will double, that deserts will expand and forests disappear, and that at least half the world's oil will be depleted. That is, if the present system should survive that long!

[5] What have individual nations, or even the United Nations, been able to do about this crisis? Very little, as yet. It all shows how urgently we need God's kingdom!

4, 5. (a) What other problems touch our lives? (b) What world trends show that it is urgent for 'God's kingdom to come'?

DOES MANKIND NEED GOD'S KINGDOM?

"If a one-megaton nuclear device were exploded over New York City, it would probably kill 2.25 million people immediately, seriously injure an additional 3.6 million, . . . a group of physicians and nuclear physicists agreed yesterday. . . . Their belief is that the world will experience such a war before the century is over and that it would make the continued existence of humans impossible."—New York "Times," September 27, 1980

WHAT IS THAT KINGDOM?

6 Is it simply a condition centered within the hearts of believers? In other words, when enough people are converted to Christianity, will God's kingdom be here? Some persons have reasoned that way, pointing to Luke 17:21 in the King James Version, or Authorized Version, of the Bible (in English), which says: "The kingdom of God is within you." But if their conclusion is correct, the kingdom of God is getting ever farther away. Why? Because the proportion of professed Christians to others in the world today is less than 25 percent, and is diminishing. Also, there are hundreds of millions of church members who seldom go inside a church.

7 Think, too, about this: To whom was Jesus talking when he said, "The kingdom of God is within you"? It was to the hypocritical Pharisees that Jesus applied God's words by the prophet Isaiah: "Their heart is far from me." (Matthew 15:1, 8, *AV*; Isaiah 29:13) How could the Kingdom enter into those hard hearts? What, then, is the meaning of Jesus' words? There is a clue in editions of the *King James Version* that have marginal readings. There the alternative reading given is: "The kingdom of God is among you." And this is the way that many other translations of the Bible, such as the Catholic *Jerusalem Bible* and *The New English Bible*, also read.

8 So, then, Jesus was here speaking of himself, the King-designate, as being among them. He was actually there in their midst, as a real person. And

6. Why would we be due for disappointment if God's kingdom were only in the hearts of people?
7, 8. How does an examination of the Scriptures help us to arrive at the true meaning of Luke 17:21?

this should bring home to us, too, that the Kingdom is a real kingdom, an actual government, even as its King is an actual person.

THE REALITY TODAY

[9] Today, few kingdoms remain on this earth. They are real governments, including Norway, the United Kingdom, Jordan and Nepal, to name some of them. In these there is a king (or a queen), together with associated rulers who serve as a parliament, diet or other governmental body. Under this comparatively small ruling group, the masses of the people go about their daily lives. They are the subjects of the kingdom.

[10] Where the king and his corulers are deeply concerned about the people's welfare, a kingdom can provide many benefits. It was that way in the ancient kingdom of Solomon, when the people "were many, like the grains of sand that are by the sea for multitude, eating and drinking and rejoicing."—1 Kings 4:20; 10:1-9.*

[11] Does the fact that the kingdom of God rules from heaven make it any less real? Why, no! In the first place, it has a king who is very much alive and active. He is God's own appointee, the Lord Jesus Christ, of whom the Bible says: "On him nations will rest their hope." (Romans 15:12) Like governments on earth, the heavenly kingdom has a

---

* Unless otherwise indicated, all scriptures quoted in part or in full in this book are quoted from the *New World Translation of the Holy Scriptures*, published by the producers of this book.

9, 10. What is a real kingdom, and how can it benefit its subjects?
11. In what ways is the kingdom of God similar to kingdoms on earth?

composite ruling body. The Bible shows this to be made up of a limited number of associate kings, who have proved their integrity to God as men and women upon this earth. To these, Jesus says: "Have no fear, little flock, because your Father has approved of giving you the kingdom." (Luke 12:32; Revelation 5:9, 10; 20:4) The kingdom has heavenly authority. From its vantage point in the heavens, the Kingdom government can project its commands —by means far more powerful than radio or laser beams—to any place on earth.

[12] What about laws? Yes, God's kingdom operates by laws—the very best of laws, made by God to benefit the people. You can read about them in the Bible. (Deuteronomy 6:4-9; Mark 12:28-31) Does the Kingdom have an educational system? Certainly it does! Right now its educational program is reaching out to aid sincere persons of all nations and peoples and languages, to prepare them for life eternal under the Kingdom's righteous administration. In whatever country of earth you may live, you personally can avail yourself of this course of instruction.—Matthew 24:14; Revelation 7:9, 10; Isaiah 54:13.

[13] Does the Kingdom have a health program? It has the most practical of all health programs—that based on the ransom sacrifice of the Lord Jesus Christ. This program will rid humans of their ailments and physical weaknesses, so that they may attain to everlasting life in the fullness of good health. (Isaiah 25:8; John 10:10) While he was on earth, Jesus performed many miracles, illustrating that he would have the authority and power to

---

12, 13. God's kingdom has what kind of (a) laws, (b) educational arrangement, (c) health program?

cure the sick, restore sight to the blind, heal the lame, and even bring dead persons back to life. (Luke 7:20-23) While this Kingdom program lies yet in the future, those who are learning about it today are learning also to lead clean, moral lives and are being restored right now to radiant spiritual health. Their hope is a real one.—Isaiah 65:14; Romans 10:11.

[14] When Jesus was a man on earth, he taught many things about the kingdom of God and, in fact, provided a preview of life under its rulership. (Luke 4:43; Matthew 12:22-28) He taught his disciples about God, so that they could draw close to God in the relationship of sons to a loving father. He provided them with sound guidance for coping successfully with the situations we encounter in life.—John 1:18; 14:6.

THE SOURCE OF TRUE HAPPINESS

[15] The prayer for 'God's kingdom to come' is part of the Sermon on the Mount, which Jesus gave on a hillside overlooking the Sea of Galilee. His listen-

---

14. While on earth, what did Jesus feature in his teaching?
15. Why were the people of Jesus' day like us today in needing comfort?

THE REALITY OF GOD'S KINGDOM

KING: Jesus, with authority to rule for 1,000 years.
HEAVENLY CORULERS: Chosen by God from faithful humans.
ITS REALM: Our earth with global paradise to be restored.
LOYAL SUBJECTS: Billions, to include resurrected dead.
LAWS: Based on God's righteousness, kingly law of love.
EDUCATIONAL PROGRAM: Aiding persons of all races to enjoy a happy life now, and preparing them for everlasting life in the earthly paradise.

ers were his chosen disciples, along with crowds of other people. These had been "skinned and thrown about" by selfish men. (Matthew 9:36) What Jesus said brought comfort to his hearers, and his words can be just as comforting to us today.

[16] Jesus started his sermon by pointing to the source of true happiness. Was this to be found in material wealth, in entertainment, in seeking thrills and excitement? No, for Jesus placed the emphasis on spiritual things. He showed that persons who are "conscious of their spiritual need" and who are "hungering and thirsting for righteousness" would find lasting happiness in connection with God's kingdom. (Matthew 5:3, 6; Luke 8:1, 4-15) Are you cultivating such spiritual interests?

[17] In the course of his sermon, Jesus made it plain that, to be approved by God, we must learn to be imitators of our heavenly Father. We should reflect his qualities and conduct ourselves according to his standards. (Matthew 5:43-48; Ephesians 5:1, 2) To please him our worship cannot be some mere formalism that we go through once or twice a week. It must be a living, active worship, that is reflected in our daily lives and in our loving concern for fellow humans.

[18] However, if we place spiritual values first in our lives, will this not lead to our suffering want in today's greedy, self-seeking society? Not at all! If we 'seek first God's kingdom and his righteousness,' then all other necessary things of life will be added

16. Who are the ones that find true happiness, and how?
17, 18. (a) What must we do to be approved by God? (b) How does Jesus' assurance at Matthew 6:26-33 appeal to you?

to us. Jesus explains this beautifully at Matthew 6:26-33, which you should read.

[19] How, then, are we to 'seek first the kingdom'? Does it mean that if we 'go to the church of our choice' we will surely receive God's blessing? Or do we need to seek out the kind of worship that God chooses for us? Note what Jesus said about this: "Not everyone saying to me, 'Lord, Lord,' will enter into the kingdom of the heavens, but the one doing the will of my Father who is in the heavens will." He made clear that some who claimed 'to have prophesied in his name and to have done powerful works in his name' would actually be "workers of lawlessness" from God's standpoint. (Matthew 7:21-23; see also 7:13, 14.) How can we know for sure how God views our worship? Only by getting well acquainted with what is contained in his Word, the Bible.

[20] An examination of the Bible will help us to give God's kingdom the prominence it deserves in our lives, and in a way that fits our individual circumstances. It will assist us to take a fresh view of life, and to appreciate what the most important things are. So let us consider next that part of Jesus' Sermon on the Mount known as "the Lord's Prayer." (Matthew 6:9-13) A review of this Model Prayer will help us to get a true perspective on what God requires of us if we are to find true happiness. And it will show us that the thrilling theme of the Bible is the sanctifying of God's name by his kingdom in the hands of Jesus Christ.

19, 20. (a) Why is it important to know how God views our worship? (b) How may we be helped to give God's kingdom prominence in our lives? (c) Why will it be profitable to review "the Lord's Prayer"?

CHAPTER 2

THE KING OF ETERNITY

JESUS opened "the Lord's Prayer" by addressing God as "our Father." No, not just the Father of Jesus Christ, but eventually the Father of all mankind who obediently worship this loving "Hearer of prayer." (Psalm 65:2) As "King of eternity" he displays a genuine and lasting concern for his creatures, even as a fine human father does for his children. (1 Timothy 1:17) We should have confidence in "our Father" as a real Person who cares for us. Whatever our language, skin color or station in life, we should feel free to approach him, for "God is not partial, but in every nation the man that fears him and works righteousness is acceptable to him."—Acts 10:34, 35.

[2] "Our Father in the heavens" is the Creator, the One who gave life to humankind. (Matthew 6:9; Psalm 36:9) But he is much more than our Life-Giver; he is also our Grand Provider. We would expect a responsible human father to provide home and sustenance for his children, even at the cost of much time and effort. Our heavenly Father has done this, and more, in a most generous way.

[3] Consider how lovingly this "King of eternity" prepared the earth to be our home. He located

---

1. Why should we have confidence in God as a real Father?
2, 3. How has our Father shown himself to be both Life-Giver and Grand Provider? (Genesis 1:1, 2, 31)

it just right in the expanse of the heavens, and by his almighty power he brought forth on earth everything necessary for happy human habitation. Then he created man and woman, placing them in this delightful home—a grand gift, indeed, "to the sons of men"!—Psalm 115:16; 19:1, 2.

[4] What a lovely home our heavenly Father provided for his children here on earth! He arranged it so that cool, restful nights could follow bright days of activity. He ordered the procession of the seasons for our benefit and pleasure. (Genesis 8:22) He supplied an abundance of that essential commodity water, and distributed it over the earth so that we might tap it wherever it was needed. He has spread a refreshing carpet of greenery—millions of square miles of it—throughout our global home. He has decorated it with exquisitely colored flowers. He has landscaped it beautifully amid a backdrop of delightful forests, lakes and mountains. In earth's "cellar" he has stored abundant supplies of coal, oil and other energy resources. He keeps replenishing earth's "larder" to overflowing with grains, fruits, vegetables and other tasty delicacies. What a wise, considerate Provider is our heavenly Father! The Bible calls him "the happy God." Obviously, he wants us to be happy, too.—1 Timothy 1:11; Isaiah 25:6-8.

OUR FATHER'S "NAME"

[5] Our loving heavenly Father has "a good name," a fine reputation as a Grand Provider. He has also

---

4. (a) What kindly foresight did our Father show in preparing our home? (b) What assures us that he wants us to be happy?
5. What should be our heart's desire in praying the opening words of Jesus' model prayer?

a personal name, just as does any human father. If we have a worthy fleshly father, we should hate to see his name and reputation reproached. We should want to see his name respected. Even more so, it should be our desire to see our heavenly Father's name honored. Therefore, from the fullness of our hearts, we should be able to pray the words that Jesus places first in the Model Prayer: "Our Father in the heavens, let your name be sanctified." —Matthew 6:9; Proverbs 22:1, footnote.

[6] Indeed, it should always be our fervent prayer that the name of the grand Creator of heaven and earth be exalted, raised on high above all other names, and shown to be the most precious, meaningful, lovable name in the universe. Far more important than our own salvation is this sanctification of God's holy name. His name and reputation must be hallowed—vindicated against all the reproach that infamous creatures have heaped upon it.

[7] What is our heavenly Father's personal name? It is revealed in a context that shows that the Owner of that grand name has enemies. In describing these, Psalm 83, verses 17 and 18, in the King James Version of the Bible, reads: "Let them be confounded and troubled for ever; yea, let them be put to shame, and perish: That men may know that thou, whose name alone is JEHOVAH, art the most high over all the earth."—See also Psalm 100:3.

[8] So, God's name is JEHOVAH. But many persons who profess to worship God have been very disre-

---

6. With regard to God's name, what would *you* like to see?
7. What does the Bible show to be God's personal name?
8. What have God's enemies tried to do with his name, and with what result?

spectful of that name. Some have even purged his name from their translations of the Bible, substituting therefor the titles "LORD" and "GOD" in all capital letters. This practice not only hides God's illustrious name, but also confuses the Lord Jehovah with the Lord Jesus Christ and with other "lords" and "gods" referred to in the Bible. (Psalm 110:1; Deuteronomy 10:17; Romans 1:4; 1 Corinthians 8:5, 6) How can persons pray honestly for the Father's name to be hallowed, or sanctified, when they seek to bury that name?

[9] The peerless name of God is represented in Hebrew, the first language used in Bible writing, by the characters יהוה, which some pronounce Yah′weh. The generally accepted form of the name in English is "Jehovah," and the name is similarly represented in other tongues. By using the name "Jehovah" we are able to indicate clearly who is meant. He is "one Jehovah." He is not Jesus Christ, for Jesus is God's loyal Son, "the image of the invisible God, the firstborn of all creation."—Colossians 1:15; Mark 12:29; Deuteronomy 6:4.

[10] The name "Jehovah" has powerful meaning. It signifies: "He Causes to Become (or, Prove to Be)." This is with regard to Himself, not with respect to His creating things. Thus, he declared "Jehovah" to be his own "memorial" name when he was about to become the miraculous Deliverer of his people Israel from Pharaoh of Egypt. (Exodus 3:13-15) Later, when the prophet Jeremiah acknowledged the Sovereign Lord Jehovah to be the Maker of heaven

9. (a) What form does God's name take in Hebrew, and in other tongues? (b) The Bible shows God to be how many persons?
10. What does God's name mean, and how has he demonstrated this?

and earth 'by his great power and his outstretched arm,' and as "great in counsel and abundant in acts," Jehovah assured his prophet that, in His own due time, He would perform a seemingly impossible act by becoming the Restorer of His people from captivity to the Babylonian Empire. And he did! —Jeremiah 32:17-19, 27, 44; 2 Chronicles 36:15-23.

[11] Today, also, Jehovah is the great God who "causes to become." He is able personally to become whatever is required, to fill any needed role, in order to perform wonderful things by means of his kingdom, in sanctifying his name and for the benefit of his people. Whatever he purposes to do *is done*, with success.—Isaiah 48:17; 55:11.

GOD'S NAME SANCTIFIED?

[12] Has mankind shown appreciation, respect and love for this illustrious God, who is so upright and who has provided so wonderfully for his creatures on earth? Look around this globe, and you will see the answer. How woefully God has been misrepresented by the religions of so-called Christian nations! Many of these nations have seen him as a partisan God, and have prayed for him to help them in warring against their fellowmen. Others have regarded him as a fiendish God, who consigns "departed souls" to agonizing flames of eternal torment. Still others have degraded him by likening him to lifeless images of wood or stone. Many have willfully violated his righteous laws, saying that God no longer sees or cares.—Contrast Acts 10:34, 35; Jeremiah 7:31; Isaiah 42:8 and 1 Peter 5:7.

---

11. How may God's name be linked today with his kingdom?
12. How has mankind regarded God?

[13] However, if misguided persons do not love God and sanctify his name, how are they going to love their fellowmen? (1 John 4:20, 21; 5:3) And unless love is restored among the family of mankind, the world must at last become a jungle of disunity, violence and anarchy. In some places, it is that way already. With the spread of nuclear armaments among the nations, someday trigger-happy persons could annihilate the entire human race. But that is something our loving Father will never permit! —Psalm 104:5; 119:90; Isaiah 45:18.

HOW GOD SANCTIFIES HIS NAME

[14] Who is it that takes the lead in sanctifying God's name? Why, it is Jehovah himself! This he does by acting in vindication of his righteous standards. He will execute judgment on all who defy his holy will, including those who oppress their fellowmen and those who teach falsehoods about God. (Psalm 140:12, 13; Jeremiah 25:29-31) Jehovah cannot deny himself. He is the true God, who deserves the exclusive worship of all his creatures. He is the Universal Sovereign, to whom all creatures owe obedience.—Romans 3:4; Exodus 34:14; Psalm 86:9.

[15] In sanctifying his name, the Sovereign Lord Jehovah will rid this earth of all humans who act ruinously, contrary to his will. This is because he hates wickedness and loves righteousness. (Psalm 11:5-7) As he himself says: "I shall certainly magnify myself and sanctify myself and make myself known before the eyes of many nations; and they will have to know that I am Jehovah." (Ezekiel

---

13. What would be the final result if misguided persons were permitted to pursue their unloving ways?
14, 15. Who takes the lead in sanctifying God's name, and how?

38:23) Clearly, then, if we want to enjoy Jehovah's approval, we too must sanctify his name, treating it as holy and deserving of full respect, and live in harmony with his will.

[16] The conduct of all who worship Jehovah either honors the name of God or dishonors it. May all of us conduct ourselves in a way that causes others to speak well of the grand God that we serve and that brings joy to Jehovah's own heart. (1 Peter 2:12; Proverbs 27:11) As obedient children, we should want to show thankfulness to our Father for all his gifts, including our delightful home—the earth—which will be restored to even greater glory under the Kingdom rule of his Son.—Isaiah 6:3; 29:22, 23.

[17] How desirable it is that we come into an approved relationship with this "King of eternity"! However, we cannot do this on our own merit, for all of us were conceived by sinful parents and brought forth imperfect. But we can pray to God as did King David: "Conceal your face from my sins, and wipe out even all my errors. Create in me even a pure heart, O God, and put within me a new spirit, a steadfast one." (Psalm 51:5-10) As we learn what "our Father in the heavens" requires of us, we can pray for a share in the eternal blessings that his kingdom will bring. Yes, confidently we can pray for God's kingdom to come. And what will that kingdom mean for mankind here on earth? Let us see.

---

16. What part does our conduct play in sanctifying God's name?
17. With what attitude should we approach the "King of eternity" in prayer?

CHAPTER 3

WHAT THE KINGDOM MEANS FOR OUR EARTH

JESUS' model prayer continues with these words: "Let your kingdom come. Let your will take place, as in heaven, also upon earth." (Matthew 6:10) God is deeply concerned with our earth, and with all who live and who have lived here. That is why the Kingdom *comes*, to "bring to ruin those ruining the earth," to provide for the resurrection of the dead, to remove the enemy death and to make our globe a happy, peaceful home for mankind's habitation.—Revelation 11:15, 18; 21:1, 3, 4.

[2] How eagerly, then, we should pray those words, "Let your kingdom come"! This is God's kingdom in the hands of his Son, the Lord Jesus Christ. By means of it the will of Jehovah, who is himself the "King of eternity," shall indeed be carried out on this earth. Consider what that will mean for the people of all nations:

THE "PRINCE OF PEACE" RULES

[3] Looking forward to Christ's Kingdom rule, God's

1, 2. How does the coming of the Kingdom show that God cares for earth and its people?
3, 4. (a) Despite taking what prophetic words to itself has the U.N. failed, and why? (b) What agency alone can provide lasting peace, and by what means?

prophet describes him as the "Prince of Peace," and adds, "To the abundance of the princely rule and to peace there will be no end." The same prophet assures us: "They shall beat their swords into plowshares, and their spears into pruninghooks: nation shall not lift up sword against nation, neither shall they learn war any more." Though these last words are inscribed on the plaza wall across the street from the United Nations, it is not that strife-torn international body that fulfills the prophecy. For the U.N. has failed dismally as an organ for establishing peace and security among nations. —Isaiah 2:4, *AV*; 9:6, 7, *NW*.

4 True and lasting peace requires that there be justice for everyone, a real practice of righteousness. Only the kingdom of the "Prince of Peace" can guarantee this; it will be 'firmly established and sustained by means of righteousness.' Yes, that kingdom is God's agency for providing "upon earth peace among men of goodwill."—Isaiah 9:7; 32:17; Luke 2:14.

5 How will the Kingdom do this? It will be, outstandingly, through the 'coming' of God's kingdom by his "Prince of Peace" against the warring nations of the world. Psalm 46:8, 9 invites us: "Behold the activities of Jehovah, how he has set astonishing events on the earth. He is making wars to cease to the extremity of the earth. The bow he breaks apart and does cut the spear in pieces; the [war] wagons he burns in the fire." The Kingdom will outlaw all weapons of violence. Moreover, it will not permit wicked thugs and rapists to stalk the streets, for under God's kingdom "the meek ones themselves

---

5. In establishing real peace, what astonishing things does the Kingdom accomplish?

will possess the earth, and they will indeed find their exquisite delight in the abundance of peace." —Psalm 37:9-11.

A PROPHETIC ILLUSTRATION

[6] Many prophecies of the Bible have reference to the captivity of Israel of old. After serving Babylon for 70 years, a faithful remnant of Israelites returned to their own land in 537 B.C.E. All those years, the land had lain in desolation, a wilderness. But now, with Jehovah's blessing on his people, there was a remarkable transformation. Prophecy written hundreds of years in advance came to glorious fulfillment:

"The wilderness and the waterless region will exult, and the desert plain will be joyful and blossom as the saffron. Without fail it will blossom, and it will really be joyful with joyousness and with glad crying out. The glory of Lebanon itself must be given to it, the splendor of Carmel and of Sharon. There will be those who will see the glory of Jehovah, the splendor of our God."—Isaiah 35:1, 2; see also Isaiah 65:18-25; Micah 4:4.

[7] As history testifies, these prophecies had a marvelous fulfillment toward God's restored people during the century following their release from Babylon. And when God's kingdom 'comes' for the blessing of *all* of God's children here on earth, will it do any less in restoring paradisaic conditions to our globe? The answer is a resounding No! The Kingdom will indeed see that God's original mandate to mankind to 'subdue the earth,' making all

---

6. What glorious fulfillment did Bible prophecy have in the sixth century B.C.E.?
7. What, then, can we expect for our earth when God's kingdom 'comes'?

of it into an Edenic paradise, will be carried out to completion.—Genesis 1:28; 2:8-14; Isaiah 45:18.

A GLOBAL PARADISE

[8] When God's kingdom 'comes,' food shortages and inflation will disappear, for "there will come to be plenty of grain on the earth; on the top of the mountains there will be an overflow." Our loving Father will again "cause food to go forth from the earth, and wine that makes the heart of mortal man rejoice, to make the face shine with oil, and bread that sustains the very heart of mortal man." (Psalm 72:16; 104:14, 15) There will be no problems of food distribution among nations, no rationing, no lining up for fuel supplies. Greedy profiteers will be gone. All mankind will obey the kingly law, "You must love your neighbor as yourself," sharing with one another according to the need.—James 2:8.

[9] Moreover, we can expect that the Kingdom will control natural upheavals, such as earthquakes and hurricanes. Jesus indicated how this could be done when he stilled "a great violent windstorm." Thus, his disciples took note that "even the wind and the sea obey him." (Mark 4:37-41) In all the earthly realm of God's kingdom, there will be nothing that hurts, harms or brings to ruin.—Compare Isaiah 11:6-9.

[10] No longer will large hospitals be needed to house the physically and mentally sick. Heart dis-

---

8. Under the Kingdom, what will happen to food and fuel supplies, and because of the application of what law?
9. What assurance do we have that nothing will then harm mankind?
10. What did Jesus' many miracles indicate with regard to the Kingdom?

WHAT GOD'S KINGDOM WILL DO

- Uphold Jehovah's sovereignty, end Satan's rule.
- Rid earth of false religion and oppressive rulers.
- Bring in Christ's reign as "Prince of Peace."
- Cause all earth to blossom as a glorious paradise.
- Remove all shortages of housing, food and fuel.
- Establish society on basis of neighbor love.
- Control earth's natural forces, prevent disasters.
- Eliminate stresses, worries, aches, pains, old age.
- Destroy the enemy death, sickness and all sorrow.
- Raise the dead billions, to live forever on earth.

ease, cancer and other crippling illnesses will be eradicated, for the Master Physician, Jesus Christ, will apply the value of his ransom sacrifice "for the curing of the nations." Jesus' many miracles of healing and raising the dead, performed while he was on earth, are only a small indication of what he will accomplish by his powerful Kingdom rule. Even mankind's inherited dying condition will be removed, for we are assured that "death will be no more."—Revelation 21:4; 22:1, 2; Matthew 11:2-5; Mark 10:45; Romans 5:18, 19.

[11] And joy of joys!—cemeteries will no longer mar the landscape, for even these will have been emptied. A "firstfruits" of the resurrection, 144,000 loyal disciples of Jesus, are to be united with him in the heavens as his associates in his kingdom. There will also be fulfilled Jesus' marvelous promise that the rest of the dead "in the memorial tombs will hear his voice and come out . . . to a resurrection." These will have the delightful opportunity to be brought to human perfection as subjects of the

11. During Jesus' Kingdom rule, what joy will cap it all?

Kingdom here on earth.—John 5:28, 29; Revelation 14:1-5; 20:4-6, 11, 12.

[12] Do you wish to be one of those who will live to see this earth cleansed of all wickedness and transformed into a paradise of pleasure? Do you wish to be here to welcome back the resurrected dead? Would you like to live forever on an earth made glorious—where no one grows weak with age or ever tires of the delights that come with each day of life? You may, if you follow God's requirements for gaining life. Jesus put it simply, when he said in prayer to his Father: "This means everlasting life, their taking in knowledge of you, the only true God, and of the one whom you sent forth, Jesus Christ." (John 17:3) What a privilege it will be to live eternally in paradise, when "the earth will be filled with the knowing of the glory of Jehovah as the waters themselves cover over the sea"!—Habakkuk 2:14.

"OUR BREAD FOR THIS DAY"

[13] However, we today are deeply concerned with present needs. For many of us, making a living and providing for our families have become a real challenge. So we need not only to pray for the Father to sanctify his great name and cause his will to be done on earth through the coming of his kingdom; we need also to pray to God for our daily necessities, for "our bread for this day." This we can do with full confidence that, if we endeavor to live according to God's righteous principles and

12. (a) Why should you want to live eternally in paradise? (b) According to John 17:3, what must we do in order to be there?
13. Why may we confidently pray for "our bread for this day"?

keep the interests of his kingdom first in our lives, God will do his part as the Great Provider. It is just as Jesus goes on to tell us: "Never be anxious and say, 'What are we to eat?' or, 'What are we to drink?' or, 'What are we to put on?' For all these are the things the nations are eagerly pursuing. For your heavenly Father knows you need all these things. Keep on, then, seeking first the kingdom and his righteousness, and all these other things will be added to you."—Matthew 6:11, 31-33.

"FORGIVE US OUR DEBTS"

[14] In building an intimate relationship with our Father, we need humbly to recognize our indebtedness to him, and to acknowledge our trespasses against God and our fellowmen. Appropriate it is, then, to pray to God: "Forgive us our debts, as we also have forgiven our debtors."—Matthew 6:12.

[15] As a marvelous kindness, completely undeserved on our part, God sent his Son, Jesus, into the world, so that he might "give his soul a ransom in exchange for many" of us humans. This provides a basis for forgiving our sins. (Matthew 20:28) How great is God's mercy thus displayed to sinful mankind! What compelling reason we have, then, for overlooking the weaknesses of our fellowmen! We should be ready to go even farther than that: to *forgive* even serious sins against us. In this way we can display toward others that quality of intense love that Jesus said would be an identifying mark of true Christians.—John 13:35; Colossians 3:13; 1 Peter 1:22.

14, 15. (a) In praying the words of Matthew 6:12, how should we be ready to act? (b) In this, what marvelous examples may we imitate?

"DELIVER US FROM THE WICKED ONE"

[16] Finally, Jesus instructs us to pray to God: "Do not bring us into temptation, but deliver us from the wicked one." (Matthew 6:13) Let us not think that God places temptations in our path, causing us to fall. Rather, it is that wicked rebel against God, Satan, who wants to turn us away from God.

[17] However, the Father equips us to "stand firm against the machinations of the Devil," yes, to wrestle successfully with him and the wicked spirit forces that he controls. So that we may not be 'brought into temptation,' God provides us a complete suit of spiritual armor, which we may put on. The apostle Paul describes it at Ephesians 6:10-18. As we stand firm in using this God-given equipment, carrying on prayer, the Father will see to it that we are 'not brought into temptation,' but are 'delivered from the wicked one.'—1 Peter 5:6-9.

[18] May Jehovah's illustrious name be sanctified soon through the 'coming of his kingdom.' May his will be done on earth by the clearing out of all badness and by making this a global paradise to his praise. As long as the present evil system lasts, may our loving heavenly Father provide us the necessities of life, help us to maintain fine relations with others and deliver us from Satan's clutches. These are the things for which Jesus taught us to pray. His model prayer contains it all.

16, 17. (a) How are we to understand the words, "Do not bring us into temptation"? (b) How may we act in harmony with the prayer 'to be delivered from the wicked one'?
18. In summary, what is the content of the Model Prayer?

CHAPTER 4

THE KINGDOM 'COMES' —FROM WHERE?

SINCE the Bible describes Jehovah as the "King of eternity," why does a kingdom have to "come" to sanctify his name? (1 Timothy 1:17; Revelation 15:3) And from where does it come?

[2] In the first place, it is obvious that some sweeping change must take place in order to restore righteousness, peace and happiness to this earth. Not only have individual governments in many ways failed to care for the welfare of their citizens, but the nations are in turmoil among themselves. Hatreds, rivalries and nationalistic prejudices divide people and races. These conditions grossly misrepresent the purpose of the Creator and have caused much reproach to be heaped upon his name.—Romans 2:24; Ezekiel 9:9.

[3] To correct this situation, a very special government is needed. And that is what Jehovah provides. From where does it come? From Jehovah himself,

---

1. On the basis of 1 Timothy 1:17 and Revelation 15:3, what important questions are raised?
2. What conditions in government have brought reproach on God's name, and in what way?
3. (a) How does God's kingdom "come" into this picture? (b) What is so special about the Kingdom?

who dwells in the heavens. It is a dependent kingdom that expresses Jehovah's own universal sovereignty. It derives its authority from the kingship that Jehovah has exercised from the beginning, long before our heavens and earth were created. Since it is born from God's heavenly organization, this very special divine government inherits the marvelous characteristics of Jehovah's agelong sovereignty. —Revelation 12:1, 2, 5.

JEHOVAH'S UNIVERSAL SOVEREIGNTY

[4] Because he "created all things" God is the rightful Sovereign over all existing creation. Even those whom God exalts to kingship in the heavens must "fall down before the One seated upon the throne and worship the One that lives forever and ever." These humbly acknowledge the supreme sovereignty of the "King of eternity"—as shown by this further description of them:

> ***"And they cast their crowns before the throne, saying: 'You are worthy, Jehovah, even our God, to receive the glory and the honor and the power, because you created all things, and because of your will they existed and were created.'" (Revelation 4:10, 11; Ephesians 3:9)***

Is that the way you view God's sovereignty? It should be.

[5] Among humans a kingdom governs according to law. This is necessary for maintaining order. Usually, governments include judges who try cases at law, parliaments to make the statutes of the law, and a king or a president who administers the

---

4. What expression at Revelation 4:11 aptly describes Jehovah's sovereignty?

5. In comparison with human governments, how is Jehovah's kingship all-embracing?

law. In the universe that he created, Jehovah God fills all three of such offices, as the prophet Isaiah indicates, saying: "Jehovah is our Judge, Jehovah is our Statute-giver, Jehovah is our King." (Isaiah 33:22) And to this King David adds the words: "Jehovah himself has firmly established his throne in the very heavens; and over everything his own kingship has held domination." (Psalm 103:19) Let us examine some aspects of that kingship.

GOD'S UNIVERSAL LAWS

[6] Governments of men seek to regulate the actions of their human subjects, but they cannot control the forces of nature that so profoundly affect their lives. Jehovah, the Universal Sovereign, can, and he does. Men of science have often marveled at the exactness of the laws by which the physical universe keeps running. These are laws of God. It is because such laws apply without variation that men have been able to land on the moon, communicate through satellites, forecast eclipses and bring forth thousands of intricate inventions. God's laws also control the sun and the rain, and he can regulate these for the blessing of those who obey him.—Psalm 89:8, 11-13; Job 38:33, 34; Zechariah 14:17.

[7] With reference to the stupendous array of heavenly bodies, God's prophet says: "Raise your eyes high up and see. Who has created these things? It is the One who is bringing forth the army of them even by number, all of whom he calls even by name. Due to the abundance of dynamic energy,

---

6. What demonstrates the superiority of God's laws?
7. (a) How do Jehovah's laws testify to his godship? (b) Like Job, how should we regard God's ways?

he also being vigorous in power, not one of them is missing. Have you not come to know or have you not heard? Jehovah, the Creator of the extremities of the earth, is a God to time indefinite." (Isaiah 40:26, 28) Through billions of years Jehovah has controlled his vast universe by so-called "natural" laws. Humans have tried to unlock the secrets of these laws, but there is so much they have yet to learn! They have advanced little farther than that faithful man of 3,500 years ago, who declared: "Look! These are the fringes of his ways, and what a whisper of a matter has been heard of him! But of his mighty thunder who can show an understanding?"—Job 26:14.

[8] However, in creating our earth, Jehovah did much more than establish it on the basis of his physical laws. His fathomless wisdom and immeasurable love were blended in with his power and his laws, in making marvelous preparation for earth's future inhabitants. What kindly foresight, what masterful skill, is to be observed in God's creative works here on earth! (1 John 4:8; Psalm 104:24; 145:3-5, 13) As we noted in an earlier chapter, Jehovah is indeed the Grand Provider!

[9] We should be thankful to God for all of his marvelous provisions. Also, we should thank him for the way he designed and made us humans, with our physical and mental abilities and our senses whereby we may find delight in his creations. Yes, we should be ready to acknowledge to God, as did the psalmist: "I shall laud you because in a fear-

---

8. What other qualities of God blend in, showing him to be a Grand Provider?
9. What are some of the things for which we should thank God?

inspiring way I am wonderfully made. Your works are wonderful, as my soul is very well aware. My bones were not hidden from you when I was made in secret, when I was woven in the lowest parts of the earth. Your eyes saw even the embryo of me, and in your [design] book all its parts were down in writing, as regards the days when they were formed and there was not yet one among them." —Psalm 139:14-16.

[10] The Sovereign Lord Jehovah, who created the universe and all things in it, establishing the systems of things out of his love and wisdom, and according to his righteous laws, is also the one of whom the Bible says: "Righteousness and judgment are the established place of your throne; loving-kindness and trueness themselves come in before your face." (Psalm 89:14) Surely Jehovah is in position to bring forth a Kingdom government that will set matters right in the earth. (Psalm 40:4, 5) But how does he do this?

REVEALING A SECRET

[11] In the Bible we find many prophecies that refer to God's setting up a kingdom that will sanctify his name and cause his will to be done on earth. One of these is the prophecy of Daniel, which points to "the time of the end" when "true knowledge will become abundant." We can be happy that such knowledge is available to us today. For Daniel tells us:

---

10. What shows Jehovah to be fully capable of righting matters on earth?

11. (a) Why, today, should we be happy that true knowledge is available? (b) How may we identify "Michael," and what does his name signify?

"There will certainly occur a time of distress such as has not been made to occur since there came to be a nation until that time. And during that time your people will escape."

As Daniel states, this will be at the time when the great prince Michael stands up on behalf of God's people. The Bible identifies Michael as Jesus Christ, who wars against God's enemies in order to sanctify Jehovah's name. Appropriately, then, the name "Michael" means "Who Is Like God?" for it is Michael who proves that no one can successfully challenge Jehovah's sovereignty.—Daniel 12:1, 4; Revelation 12:7-10.

[12] The prophecy of Daniel tells also of a dream had by King Nebuchadnezzar of Babylon, a dream about a succession of kingdoms. The king promptly forgot what the dream was about, though it continued to agitate him greatly. Finally, the "Revealer of secrets," Jehovah God, used Daniel to make known to the king not only the dream but also its interpretation. (Daniel 2:29) Since the fulfillment of this prophetic dream continues right down to and beyond our day, we should be deeply interested in its meaning. The dream was about an "immense image" of human form—dreadful in appearance. You may read about it at Daniel 2:31-33. What does that image picture?

[13] Daniel made known to Nebuchadnezzar that its head of gold stood for the "king" of Babylon, and that the lower parts of its body represented other kingdoms that would arise after Babylon. Today, we can recognize these as the mighty empires of Medo-

---

12. What is the dream picture at Daniel 2:31-33, and why should it interest us today?
13. What do the various sections of the image picture?

Persia, Greece and Rome, with the "legs" extending down into the dual Anglo-American World Power of modern times. But what of the feet, made "partly of molded clay of a potter and partly of iron"? In recent years, socialistic popular movements have greatly weakened ironlike authority in the Anglo-American World Power, even as the feet of the immense image were made fragile due to the iron "not mixing with molded clay." Thus, this dreadful image represents successive human "kings," or world powers that terminate when God's kingdom destroys them.—Daniel 2:36-44.

[14] For, look! A "stone" is miraculously cut out from a mountain, "not by hands." No human physical agency is responsible for this operation. Rather, Jehovah himself brings it forth, according to his holy will. Hurtling toward the mighty image, the stone strikes it at the feet. It crushes the entire structure of human rulership, so that the remains are scattered as chaff before the wind. The stone itself then becomes a large mountain that fills the whole earth.—Daniel 2:34, 35.

[15] What could this "stone" be? The prophecy removes all doubt when it states:

"In the days of those kings [the Anglo-American World Power and the surviving remnants of the world powers that have preceded it] the God of heaven will set up a kingdom that will never be brought to ruin. And the kingdom itself will not be passed on to any other people. It will crush and put an end to all these kingdoms, and it itself will stand to times indefinite."—Daniel 2:44.

14, 15. What does the "stone" do to the image, and how can we identify that "stone"?

[16] What does this mean for us today? It means that when we pray for God's kingdom to "come," we are in fact petitioning that the heavenly kingdom use its destructive power in crushing all man-made governments, which have failed so miserably to bring in peace and prosperity. Happily, that "stone," on completing its mission of destruction, will itself grow into a governmental mountain that fills the whole earth. It will bring peace such as mankind has not known since the days of King Solomon, "the abundance of peace until the moon is no more"—which means forever!—Psalm 72:7.

[17] However, what of the "mountain" out of which this Kingdom "stone" is cut? (Daniel 2:45) The "stone" must be dependent on, and be made of the same stuff as the mountain, and indeed it is. This Kingdom rulership is cut out from the all-embracing, overall sovereignty of the King of eternity—Jehovah God. Just as the universal sovereignty of Jehovah reflects all of his fine qualities, so the kingdom that is cut out of that sovereignty must exalt Jehovah God and his grand purposes. It sanctifies his name by crushing his enemies, showing that he is not a party to their wicked deeds. Then this kingdom by Christ Jesus fills the earth with law and order, and with love and joy, transforming it into the righteous, peaceful place that God purposed from the beginning. Truly, we should be praying for 'the Kingdom to come'!—Psalm 85:8-12.

---

16. In praying, "Let your kingdom come," what things are we petitioning?
17. (a) Why should the relationship of the "stone" to the original "mountain" give us confidence? (b) What further action does the Kingdom take? (c) As stated at Psalm 85:8-12, what confidence should we have?

CHAPTER 5

THE KINGDOM—WHY SO LONG IN 'COMING'?

THE apostle Paul writes: "We know that all creation keeps on groaning together and being in pain together." (Romans 8:22) Why is this so? Why has God permitted the wars, the crime, the sickness and the misery of the past 6,000 years of recorded history? What went wrong, that humankind, created to live according to divine law, should now be plagued with lawlessness? Why has not our heavenly Father corrected this situation? If the Kingdom is the solution, why has it been so long in 'coming'? Can we really hope that God will reverse these terrible conditions?

[2] Under the supreme rulership, or sovereignty, of "the King of eternity," ideal conditions should have prevailed on earth since the time of creation in Eden. As the first man and woman brought forth children, and the human family multiplied into thousands of millions of family units, the entire earth should have become a paradise of beauty, filled with the joyful laughter and neighborly love of peaceful races of mankind.—Compare Ecclesiastes 2:24.

---

1. In view of Romans 8:22, what questions arise?
2. Under God's sovereignty, what should earth have become?

[3] That is what the loving Creator purposed for this earth when he created man after his own moral likeness and formed woman from the man. For the Bible account of creation tells us:

***"Male and female he created them. Further, God blessed them and God said to them: 'Be fruitful and become many and fill the earth and subdue it, and have in subjection the fish of the sea and the flying creatures of the heavens and every living creature that is moving upon the earth.' . . . After that God saw everything he had made and, look! it was very good."* (Genesis 1:26-31)**

Why, then, does God's creation on earth not look "very good" today?

GOD'S SOVEREIGNTY CHALLENGED

[4] Creation had as its basis God's laws. And outstanding among these is the law of love. God himself "is love." (1 John 4:8) But now someone appeared who wanted to make different laws for mankind. That "someone" was an invisible angelic 'son of God,' no doubt one of those who 'shouted in applause' when Jehovah created the earth and everything upon it. (Job 38:7) This angel turned himself into a satan, an adversary of God. He wanted to become independent, sought worship for himself and sowed a spirit of rebellion. (Ephesians 2:1, 2; compare Luke 4:5-7.) He schemed to use our first human parents for his own selfish ends. How did he go about this?

---

3. (a) In what likeness was man created? (b) What were the first human couple commissioned to do? (c) What question must we now ask?
4. (a) What law of God excels, and why? (b) Who wanted to make different laws, and how did he go about this?

[5] In the paradisaic garden of Eden, Adam and Eve were the recipients of Jehovah's benevolent rule. God provided everything necessary to sustain them spiritually and physically. For their own continuing welfare, he required also that they obey him as their Sovereign Lord. To this end he had given Adam a simple commandment, that he must not eat from "the tree of the knowledge of good and bad." This applied also to Eve, after her creation. It was not that God was depriving them of anything, for the other trees in the garden provided a delightful variety of nourishing fruits. However, if they were to disobey God in eating of this one fruit, they would "positively die." Slyly, through a serpent, the rebel Satan made his approach first to Eve, saying: "You positively will not die. For God knows that in the very day of your eating [the fruit of the tree] your eyes are bound to be opened and you are bound to be like God, knowing good and bad."—Genesis 2:17; 3:1-5.

[6] That made God appear to be a liar. But it was Satan who really was the liar. Rightly, that "father of the lie" came also to be called the Devil, meaning "Slanderer." (John 8:44) Here was a direct challenge to Jehovah's sovereignty, his Kingship over his creatures. It implied that God was withholding knowledge to which they were entitled, that God's rulership was not to be trusted, that they would do better to go their own independent way, setting their own standards of "good and bad."

[7] How did the woman respond to this slanderous

5, 6. (a) What simple command did God lay on Adam? (b) What approach did Satan make, and why is he properly called "the Devil"?

7. In what respects did the human pair fail under test?

speech? She failed to guard her heart, permitting wrong desire to take root there. This desire then became fertile, so that she was deceived into willfully committing sin by disobeying God. In this she also flouted the headship of her husband, whom she should have consulted. And how did the man react? "Adam was not deceived," but chose to throw in his lot with Eve, willfully joining her in her course of rebellion. What a sad day that was for our first parents, and for the entire race of mankind!—Genesis 3:6, 7; 1 Timothy 2:14; compare James 1:14, 15.

[8] Adam and Eve had shown gross disregard for God's sovereignty. So now, in harmony with his law, God announced the sentence of death, telling Adam:

***"For dust you are and to dust you will return."* (Genesis 3:19)**

God did not here mean that only Adam's body would die, while some inner "soul" or "spirit" escaped from the body to keep on living in a heaven or a hell. No, for Adam himself *was* a "soul." As the creation account says, at Genesis 2:7: "Jehovah God proceeded to form the man out of dust from the ground and to blow into his nostrils the breath of life, and *the man* came to be *a living soul.*" In due course, both Adam and Eve died—as souls. And because the entire human race is the offspring of the sin-tainted Adam, all of us have inherited sin and death. "The soul that is sinning—it itself will die." (Ezekiel 18:4, 20) Yes, as human souls, we all die. Death has come to rule as king over us.

---

8. (a) What just sentence did God pass on Adam and Eve? (b) Did they have souls that would go to heaven or to a hell of torment at death? (c) What king came to rule over us, and why?

—Romans 5:12, 14; 6:12; Ecclesiastes 3:19, 20; 9:5, 10; Psalm 6:5; 115:17.

THE ISSUE OF MAN'S INTEGRITY

[9] However, it was not only God's sovereignty that was called into question by the rebellion in Eden. Another issue was raised. Since the very first humans that God had placed on earth had become unfaithful under test, was there something wrong with God's creation? Could it truly be said that all his works were "perfect"?

[10] God might have destroyed Adam and Eve immediately and created another human pair. But would not that have been an admission that his first creation was defective? It was not defective. It was only that our first parents had elected to use their moral capacity of free choice in the wrong way. If they had been robots that *had* to do right under all circumstances, then they would have been lacking in a moral sense. They would not have been 'in God's likeness.' Jehovah always does things perfectly, in the right way, because he is love. He wants his intelligent creatures likewise to be motivated by love in doing what is right. —Genesis 1:26, 27; 1 John 5:3.

[11] It is written of Jehovah: "The Rock, perfect is his activity, for all his ways are justice. A God of faithfulness, with whom there is no injustice; righteous and upright is he." His creation, humankind,

9. What other issue was raised in Eden?
10. (a) Was God's creation defective, and why do you so answer? (b) How may humans show themselves to be 'in God's likeness'?
11. What light does Deuteronomy 32:4, 5 throw on the situation back there?

can also be faithful, righteous and upright. So he permitted Adam and Eve to bring forth children. Even though these inherited sinful traits from their parents, yet there would be those among them who would prove their unswerving love for their Creator and prove their integrity to him, even in their fleshly imperfection and in the face of bitter trials and persecutions that might come their way. But others of mankind would 'act ruinously' and show themselves not to be God's children. That would be their own choice, the defect being chargeable to them and not to God.—Deuteronomy 32:4, 5.

[12] That Satan the Devil pressed this issue of man's integrity before God is shown in the Bible book of Job. The man Job, who lived some 2,500 years after Adam's deflection, was "blameless and upright, fearing God and turning aside from bad." Satan taunted God that Job's uprightness was not genuine, that he served God only for what he could get out of it. So God permitted Satan to put Job to the test. Job suffered severe property losses; his 10 children were killed in a disaster; he himself was later afflicted with a loathsome disease, and finally his own wife mocked him, saying: "Are you yet holding fast your integrity? Curse God and die!" Next, Job had to contend with the sarcastic reproaches of three false comforters.—Job 1:6–2:13.

[13] Through all these trials Job held fast to his resolve:

"Until I expire I shall not take away my integrity from myself!"

He proved true to God, thus providing a strong reply

12, 13. (a) How did Satan taunt God with regard to Job? (b) What reply did Job provide, and with what result to him?

to Satan's accusations. Jehovah therefore rewarded Job by giving him double of all he had possessed before. He was also blessed in again having seven sons and three daughters—the latter being the prettiest in all the land.—Job 27:5; 42:10-15.

[14] However, Job is only one of hundreds of thousands of faithful servants of God who have made His heart rejoice because of giving an answer to Satan's false claim that lovers of Jehovah obey and serve him only for selfish reasons. The finest example of this was that of God's own Son, Jesus, who, while on earth, "endured a torture stake, despising shame," all for the joy of continuing to serve selflessly in the assignment that God gave him.—Hebrews 12:2.

THE TAUNTER'S CHALLENGE ANSWERED

[15] Now, the appointed time has nearly run out. During some 6,000 years Jehovah has been proving his side in answer to the challenge. He has shown that he *can* and *does* have men and women on earth who keep integrity no matter what persecution or other vicious trial Satan brings upon them. The Devil has used every conceivable wicked device against them, but in vain. God's faithful servants have made their Father's heart rejoice, for they have provided him with a reply to the one that is "taunting" God, namely, the great adversary, Satan. —Proverbs 27:11.

---

14. How have others likewise answered Satan's claim, and what is the finest example of this?
15. Why can it be said that Jehovah's side of the challenge has been proved?

WHY HAS GOD SO LONG PERMITTED EVIL?

- To establish the rightness, righteousness, excellence and permanence of Jehovah's universal sovereignty
- To demonstrate for all time that every kind of man-rule independent of God leads only to sorrow and disaster
- To provide for the development of God's Kingdom promises, and the selection and testing of the heirs of the Kingdom
- To allow time for proving, as in a court of law, that servants of God can keep integrity despite every trial from Satan
- To show that obedience, based on God's law of love, is the only course that leads to lasting enjoyment of life
- To answer Satan's challenge so thoroughly and to establish such a clear legal precedent that never again will it be necessary to vindicate Jehovah's name and sovereignty.

[16] At the same time, and in his economy of doing things, Jehovah has been choosing from among these loyal ones persons who will rule with Christ in the heavenly kingdom. Though Satan has accused them "day and night before our God," they have conquered him "because of the word of their witnessing, and they did not love their souls even in the face of death." Like their Exemplar, Jesus Christ, they have been willing to show the superlative quality of their love for God and neighbor by surrendering even their lives. What confidence mankind will be able to have in the heavenly kingdom made up of Christ and his 144,000 associate kings—all of them tried and proved integrity-keepers!—Revelation 12:10, 11; 14:1-5; 20:4; John 15:13.

[17] Others, such as Job, who died faithful to God

16. (a) In what conquest have certain of God's loyal ones already shared? (b) Why may the subjects of the Kingdom have confidence in their rulers?
17. Who inherit the earthly realm of the Kingdom?

in pre-Christian times, are assured of "a better resurrection" into a "new earth." (Hebrews 11:35; 2 Peter 3:13) They become part of the "other sheep" of the "fine shepherd" Jesus Christ, with the prospect of everlasting life in a paradise earth. Also, those sheeplike ones who show kindness to Christ's anointed "brothers" at the time of the "conclusion of the system of things" are invited to inherit this earthly realm of the Kingdom. (John 10:11, 16; Matthew 24:3; 25:31-46) They are saved alive when the angels of heaven unleash the winds of the "great tribulation" upon our earth. Do you want to be one of that "great crowd" of survivors when God's kingdom 'comes' to crush the wicked nations? You may be! For, as an integrity-keeper, you too may prove that God's way alone can lead to the lasting enjoyment of life.—Revelation 7:1-3, 9, 13, 14.

[18] Once God's kingdom has crushed Satan and his corrupt system of things, it will never again be necessary to vindicate God's sovereignty. The issues raised by the rebel Satan will have been answered once and for all time. (Nahum 1:9) Right here, at this earth, the rightfulness, the righteousness, the excellence of rulership based on God's law of love, will have been proved, and the Kingdom will have "come" to sanctify the grand name of the Sovereign Lord Jehovah. For those of 'groaning creation' who now serve God in integrity, what a bright hope God's kingdom holds forth! Are you praying fervently for its 'coming'?—Romans 8:22-25.

---

18. (a) Why will it never again be necessary to vindicate Jehovah's sovereignty? (b) Who now have a bright hope? (Psalm 37:11, 29)

CHAPTER 6

REACHING OUT FOR THE KINGDOM

WHEN something desirable is offered to you, how do you respond? Do you not reach out for it? Well, Jehovah God is presenting you with the opportunity of everlasting life under a perfect government. It is true that, in government today, many politicians are corrupt and their promises are often worthless. Even if they are well intentioned, humans have proved to be incapable of providing good government independent of God's sovereignty. (Proverbs 20:24) But all along, God has been taking progressive steps leading to the establishment of his perfect Kingdom government, and he invites lovers of righteousness to benefit from it. His purpose is trustworthy and true. He cannot lie. We can safely build our lives around his Word.—Revelation 21:1-5; Titus 1:2.

[2] God's purpose to establish a kingdom of righteousness is not new. In Eden, when God's sovereignty was first called in question, God stated his purpose to produce a "seed" that would "crush"

---

1. (a) With regard to government, what does Jehovah offer in contrast to what humans have provided? (b) Why may we safely build our lives around God's Word?
2. (a) When and how did God state his purpose to establish a righteous kingdom? (b) What does Hebrews 11:4-7 reveal as to those who reached out for the Kingdom hope?

Satan and his brood. (Genesis 3:15; Romans 16:20) Amid the violence of that ancient world, Abel, Enoch and Noah showed faith in that promise of Jehovah. Confident that God would reward "those earnestly seeking him," they endured reproaches, choosing to 'walk with God' and to preach righteousness. (Hebrews 11:4-7) What fine examples for all today who exercise faith in the 'coming' of God's kingdom!

A REMARKABLE FAMILY LINE

[3] More than 400 years after the Flood, God made it clear that the promised kingly "seed" would come from the family line of Abraham. But why Abraham? Because God saw in him outstanding faith. He called Abraham out of his native city, Ur of the Chaldeans, and sent him to a strange land, Canaan, saying:

> ***"All the families of the ground will certainly bless themselves by means of you, . . . to your seed I am going to give this land." (Genesis 12:3, 7; Acts 7:4)***

Rather than cling to the nation of his birth, Abraham left it, never to return. He was willing to make a complete change in his life-style, in order to render unqualified obedience to the Sovereign Lord Jehovah. A splendid model, indeed, for all who would pursue a life of dedication to Jehovah today!

[4] Though his wife, Sarah, remained barren into her old age, Jehovah later reassured Abraham, telling him: "I will bless her and she shall become

---

3. According to Genesis 12:1-7, how was Abraham a splendid model for us?
4. How was Sarah blessed because of her faith? (Hebrews 11:11, 12)

nations; kings of peoples will come from her." (Genesis 17:16) At 90 years of age, faithful Sarah was blessed in miraculously bearing Abraham a son, Isaac, the forefather of many kings.—Matthew 1:2, 6-11, 16; Revelation 17:14.

[5] In the course of time, Jehovah put both Abraham and Isaac to a searching test. He instructed Abraham to take his only son by Sarah some three days' journey to Mount Moriah, there to sacrifice him as a burnt offering. By now Isaac quite likely was about 25 years of age and strong enough to carry the heavy load of firewood up the mountain; strong enough also to resist his 125-year-old father, had he wanted to do so. But father and son obediently acted out their parts in this stirring drama, to the point when Jehovah's angel stayed Abraham's hand as he raised the slaughtering knife. A ram replaced Isaac as the victim.—Genesis 22:1-14.

[6] Here God was making a prophetic pattern of how he would sacrifice his own Son, in order to take away the sin of the world of mankind. (John 1:29; Galatians 3:16) For God then told Abraham:

> ***"By means of your seed all nations of the earth will certainly bless themselves due to the fact that you have listened to my voice."—Genesis 22:15-18.***

[7] What outstanding examples of obedience were Abraham and Isaac! We may never be called upon to make their kind of sacrifice, but it *is* important

---

5. How was the obedience of Abraham and Isaac rewarded?
6. (a) What prophetic pattern was there enacted? (b) Why should the promise at Genesis 22:18 be of special interest to you?
7. What course on our part will Jehovah reward?

that we submit ourselves to Jehovah as they did, out of genuine love for him. (James 4:7; 2 Corinthians 9:13) Willingness to sacrifice self and selfish interests, in order to reach out for 'the Kingdom to come,' is a course that Jehovah always approves and rewards.—Matthew 6:33.

[8] Isaac's son Jacob was another person who reached out for the Kingdom. But his twin brother Esau despised sacred things, getting interested in Canaanite women and in selfish materialism. And he sold his precious birthright to Jacob for a mere dish of stew! (Hebrews 12:16) The spiritually minded Jacob thought highly of the birthright, and Jehovah directed matters so that he could retain that prize, even to receiving the aged Isaac's blessing. Esau had married demon-worshiping women, but in contrast Jacob made the long journey to Mesopotamia to seek a wife from among Jehovah's worshipers. At that time Isaac reassured Jacob with the words:

"God Almighty will bless you and make you fruitful and multiply you, and you will certainly become a congregation of peoples."—Genesis 25:27-34; 26:34, 35; 27:1-23; 28:1-4.

[9] Later, when he was close to 100 years of age, Jacob again showed how highly he valued spiritual things. He wrestled with an angel all night for a blessing. As a token of His favor, Jehovah there changed Jacob's name to Israel, meaning "Perseverer with God." (Genesis 32:24-30) We will be

---

8. (a) How did the course of Jacob contrast with that of Esau? (b) What blessing did Isaac bestow on Jacob?
9. (a) Why was Jacob's name changed to Israel? (b) How may we benefit from his example?

rewarded today, also, if we persevere in reaching out for spiritual riches, while avoiding the spirit of the wicked world around us.—Matthew 6:19-21.

[10] Jehovah did indeed organize Jacob's descendants as a "congregation of peoples," and through His mediator Moses, whom He used also to start writing down the Bible, God called to that nation of Israel, saying:

"If you will strictly obey my voice . . . you yourselves will become to me a kingdom of priests and a holy nation." (Exodus 19:5, 6)

Unhappily, because of *not* obeying God's voice, fleshly Israel failed to become that spiritual kingdom. But in association with that nation, many individuals proved their integrity to God—such as the judges in Israel, the prophets and even a former harlot, Rahab. We can read about those faithful "witnesses" at Hebrews 11:1–12:1, and what warm encouragement they provide for persons who are looking, in modern times, for 'God's kingdom to come'!

[11] Do you want to become strong in faith? Do you want now to be like those men and women of faith in "reaching out for a better place, that is, one belonging to heaven," yes, reaching out for "the city having real foundations, the builder and maker of which city is God"? (Hebrews 11:10, 16) 'But,' you may ask, 'what is that "city"?'

---

10. (a) How was the prophecy at Genesis 28:3 fulfilled? (b) As to individual faithfulness, what are some of the heartwarming examples at Hebrews 11:1–12:1?
11. How may you be like those faithful witnesses?

THE CITY BUILT BY GOD

[12] That "city" is the promised kingdom of God. Why do we say so? Well, in ancient times it was often true that a city was a kingdom, ruled over by a king. The first king mentioned with approval in the Bible was "Melchizedek, king of [the city of] Salem, priest of the Most High God." Centuries later, the city of Jerusalem was built upon that same site, and, like Salem, it came to picture the heavenly kingdom in the hands of the great King and High Priest, Jesus Christ. (Genesis 14:1-20; Hebrews 7:1, 2, 15-17; 12:22, 28) Though they did not know the details then, Abraham and Sarah, as well as Isaac and Jacob, were earnestly seeking "the city" over which the Messiah would rule as king. Abraham "rejoiced greatly in the prospect." You, too, can find joy as in faith you reach out for a place in that Kingdom arrangement.—Hebrews 11:14-16; John 8:56.

[13] Jacob fathered 12 sons, who in due course became the heads of the 12 tribes of Israel. On his deathbed, Jacob foretold which of the 12 tribes would produce God's ruler with Kingdom authority, saying:

> ***"A lion cub Judah is. . . . The scepter will not turn aside from Judah . . . until Shiloh [meaning, He Whose It Is] comes; and to him the obedience of the peoples will belong." (Genesis 49:9, 10)***

Did Shiloh come from Judah? Why, yes!

[14] The fulfillment of Jacob's prophecy began to

---

12. For what "city" were those ancient servants of God reaching out? (See also Hebrews 11:22-32; Ruth 1:8, 16, 17.)
13, 14. How did Jacob's deathbed prophecy begin to have fulfillment?

THEY REACHED OUT
ABEL
c. 3900 B.C.E.
NOAH
2970-2020 B.C.E.
ABRAHAM, SARAH,
ISAAC, JACOB
2018-1711 B.C.E.
MOSES
1593-1473 B.C
JOSEPH
1767-1657 B.C.E.

FOR GOD'S KINGDOM
JOHN THE BAPTIZER
2 B.C.E.- 31 C.E.
PROPHETS
1117-442 B.C.E.
DAVID
1107-1037 B.C.E.
RUTH, NAOMI
c. 1300 B.C.E.
RAHAB
1473 B.C.E.
JUDGES
1473-1117 B.C.E.

unfold more than 600 years later. It was then that Jehovah chose, from the tribe of Judah, "a man agreeable to his heart." His name was David. God made this courageous 'lion of Judah' leader and king over His people Israel. (1 Samuel 13:14; 16:7, 12, 13; 1 Chronicles 14:17) To King David, Jehovah promised an everlasting kingdom.—Psalm 89:20, 27-29.

[15] David, who commenced his reign in 1077 B.C.E., was the first of a dynasty of Judean kings that ruled in the city of Jerusalem. The nation prospered whenever its king willingly obeyed Jehovah. But when a king became wicked and rebelled against Jehovah's righteous laws, the people suffered. (Proverbs 29:2) The last king of Judah, Zedekiah, was very wicked. To him, God's prophet declared: " 'Lift off the crown. . . . A ruin, a ruin, a ruin I shall make it . . . until he comes who has the legal right, and I must give it to him.' " The Sovereign Lord Jehovah overturned that kingdom, until a king with "legal right" would appear.—Ezekiel 21:26, 27.

THE KING WITH "LEGAL RIGHT"

[16] Who would inherit the "legal right" to the Davidic kingdom? The first 17 verses of the Bible book of Matthew supply the answer. They trace the line of the promised "seed" from Abraham to David, and then down to Joseph, who in due course became husband to Mary. Thus Mary's firstborn son would have the "legal right" to the Kingdom. Early in the year 2 B.C.E., the angel Gabriel could

---

15. Why did Jehovah overturn the Judean kingdom, and for how long?
16. How do the Scriptures identify the permanent heir of the Kingdom?

therefore announce concerning the son to be conceived miraculously in her womb:

> ***"You are to call his name Jesus. This one will be great and will be called Son of the Most High; and Jehovah God will give him the throne of David his father, and he will rule as king over the house of Jacob forever, and there will be no end of his kingdom."*** **(Luke 1:26-33)**

Grandly through the centuries Jehovah had been working out his purpose to bring forth this permanent heir to David's kingdom. As we review these things, do they not strengthen our faith in God's promise of his 'kingdom to come'?

[17] It is not that all of us can expect to be in the heavenly kingdom with Jesus, for that opportunity is reserved for only a "little flock" of his disciples. (Luke 12:32) Even King David did not have such a hope. We are told: "Actually David did not ascend to the heavens." (Acts 2:34) Nor do John the Baptizer and other faithful men and women of ancient times enter "the kingdom of the heavens." —Matthew 11:11; Hebrews 11:39, 40.

[18] However, such faithful integrity-keepers will be resurrected right here on this earth, many of them to become "princes" in God's Kingdom arrangement. (Psalm 45:16) Would you not like to welcome them back from the grave and to enjoy rich fellowship with them? Surely you would! Then be resolved, also, to reach out for that "city" by becoming "fellow workers for the kingdom of God" with all others today who appreciate that grand opportunity. —Colossians 4:11.

17, 18. (a) Who only will inherit the heavenly kingdom? (b) Who are some of the faithful ones to be resurrected on earth? (c) What should this realization encourage us to do?

CHAPTER 7

IDENTIFYING MESSIAH, THE KING

THE prophet Daniel will be among those resurrected to share in God's Kingdom arrangement on earth. As he ended his long life of service to Jehovah he was told: "You will rest, but you will stand up for your lot at the end of the days." Daniel was deeply interested in "the time of the end" and the "wonderful things" that would then happen, just as we are interested today. Therefore, it was appropriate that the great Time-Keeper, Jehovah God, use Daniel as his prophet in connection with his timetable for the 'coming' of the Kingdom.—Daniel 12:4, 6, 13; 11:27, 35; compare Amos 3:7; Isaiah 46:9-11.

"THE DEVASTATIONS OF JERUSALEM"

[2] In line with Jehovah's prophecy uttered centuries in advance, the Babylonian Empire fell before the armies of Cyrus the Persian and Darius the Mede. (Isaiah 44:24, 27, 28; 45:1, 2) Darius became king over the former Babylonian kingdom. That was in the year 539 B.C.E. Sixty-eight years had

---

1. Why, appropriately, did Jehovah use Daniel to prophesy about the timing of events?
2. (a) What prophecy of Isaiah was suddenly fulfilled in 539 B.C.E., and how? (b) What miracle was needed for Jeremiah 25:11, 12 to be fulfilled on time?

now passed since Nebuchadnezzar of Babylon had devastated Jerusalem and its temple, desolated the land of Judah and transported the surviving Jews to Babylon. It was therefore with keen anticipation that aged Daniel wrote, in the first year of Darius: "I myself, Daniel, discerned by the books the number of the years concerning which the word of Jehovah had occurred to Jeremiah the prophet, for fulfilling the devastations of Jerusalem, namely, seventy years." (Daniel 9:2; Jeremiah 25:11, 12) By what miracle could the captive Jews, within two more years, return and restore Jehovah's worship in Jerusalem?

[3] Daniel petitioned Jehovah fervently in behalf of his people, acknowledging their sins and calling on Jehovah to exercise mercy. Above all, he requested Jehovah to remove from His great name the reproach heaped upon it by Israel's neighbor nations. He entreated his God: "O Jehovah, do hear. O Jehovah, do forgive. O Jehovah, do pay attention and act. Do not delay, for your own sake, O my God, for your own name has been called upon your city and upon your people."—Daniel 9:4-19.

[4] Did Jehovah answer this prayer? He did! And in doing so, he also fulfilled his prophecy. He caused Darius' successor, Cyrus of Persia, to issue the decree for the Israelite remnant to go up to Jerusalem and rebuild Jehovah's temple. As the "seventy years" ended, in 537 B.C.E., those restored Jews began again to offer sacrifices to Jehovah at his rebuilt altar in Jerusalem.—2 Chronicles 36:17-23; Ezra 3:1; Isaiah 44:28; 45:1.

---

3. Therefore, what fervent prayer did Daniel utter?
4. How did Jehovah answer that prayer?

TIMING MESSIAH'S FIRST COMING

[5] There was also an *immediate* sequel to that prayer by Daniel. The angel Gabriel materialized before him in human form, and began speaking to him. He referred to Daniel as "someone very desirable [to Jehovah]" and proceeded to give him further "insight with understanding." (Daniel 9:20-23) What he had to say was entirely new, a fresh revelation to Daniel. It was a startling prophecy, involving events that would cover a period of, not "seventy years," but "seventy weeks." Please read it in full at Daniel 9:24-27. What does the prophecy mean?

[6] It says that "seventy weeks" had been determined with regard to the appearing of "Messiah the Leader," the promised King in the line of David. Could these be literal weeks? No, for all the things prophesied could hardly happen within a year and a half. They proved to be "weeks" in which each day counts as a year. (Compare Leviticus 25:8.) In fact, several Bible translations use expressions such as "seventy weeks of years" at Daniel 9:24. (*An American Translation, Moffatt, Today's English Version*; also see footnotes in *Rotherham, The New American Bible, The Jerusalem Bible*.) The "seventy weeks" are clearly 490 literal years.

[7] When do the "seventy weeks" begin to be counted? Daniel 9:25 tells us: "From the going forth

---

5. (a) What sequel followed immediately? (b) What time period is made prominent at Daniel 9:24-27?
6. How long are the "seventy weeks"?
7, 8. (a) Why did the "seventy weeks" not count from Cyrus' decree? (b) How was Nehemiah's prayer answered? (c) How did the Jews respond to the king's "word"? (d) When did this take place?

of the word to restore and to rebuild Jerusalem." However, Cyrus' decree contained no such "word." It was limited to 'rebuilding the house of Jehovah,' which would include the altar for sacrifice. (Ezra 1:1-4) Until more than 80 years thereafter, the city itself remained "devastated," with its walls broken down. At that time a faithful Jew, Nehemiah, was employed as cupbearer to King Artaxerxes of Persia, at the castle of Shushan. On hearing of the plight of the Jews at Jerusalem, he prayed that this "reproach" on Jehovah's name might be removed. —Nehemiah 1:3, 11; 2:17.

[8] Sad of countenance, Nehemiah brought wine to the king. Artaxerxes asked him: "Why is your face gloomy when you yourself are not sick? This is nothing but a gloominess of heart." On learning the reason, the king immediately proceeded to give Nehemiah instructions to return to Jerusalem, that he might build the "walls" and "gates" of the city. When Nehemiah arrived there to report on God's favor shown, and to convey the king's "word to restore and to rebuild Jerusalem," how did the people respond? "At this they said: 'Let us get up, and we must build.' So they strengthened their hands for the good work." All of this took place "in the twentieth year of Artaxerxes the king."—Nehemiah 2:1-18.

[9] What year was this? The weight of evidence is that this Artaxerxes (called also "Longimanus" on account of his long right hand) came to the Persian throne at the death of his father Xerxes. Artaxerxes'

---

9. How may we determine the 20th year of Artaxerxes?

first year of reigning would be 474 B.C.E. Thus his 20th year would be 455 B.C.E.*

[10] So, then, the "weeks" of Daniel 9:25 would start to count from 455 B.C.E. We read:

"And you should know and have the insight that from the going forth of the word to restore and to rebuild Jerusalem until Messiah the Leader, there will be seven weeks, also sixty-two weeks. She will return and be actually rebuilt, with a public square and moat, but in the straits of the times."

Apparently, the first "seven weeks," or 49 years, cover the time of rebuilding the city, up until 406 B.C.E. "The straits of the times" have reference to the bitter opposition this building work received from neighboring peoples. (Nehemiah 4:6-20) Nevertheless, as history indicates, Jerusalem was a large and flourishing city by the end of that century.†

[11] However, beyond this there were to be "sixty-two weeks"—making a total of 69 weeks of years, or 483 years, from 455 B.C.E. "until Messiah the Leader." These 483 years, including only part of 455 B.C.E. and part of the final year, would extend into 29 C.E. Did Messiah then appear? Luke 3:1-3 states that "in the fifteenth year of the reign of Tiberius Caesar," John the Baptizer "came into all

---

* See *The Watchtower,* October 15, 1965, pages 629-631; *Aid to Bible Understanding,* page 1473.

† For example, the fourth century B.C.E. historian Hecataeus of Abdera is quoted by Josephus in *Against Apion,* Book I:22, as writing: "The Jews have many fortresses and villages in different parts of the country, but only one fortified city, which has a circumference of fifty *stades* [about 33,000 feet] and some hundred and twenty thousand inhabitants; they call it Jerusalem."

---

10. How was the prophecy concerning the first "seven weeks" fulfilled?
11. How did "Messiah the Leader" appear right on time?

the country around the Jordan, preaching baptism." Since historians establish that Tiberius became Roman emperor on August 17, 14 C.E. (Gregorian calendar), it would follow that John's preaching and baptizing would commence during Tiberius' 15th year—in the spring of 29 C.E. In the fall of that same year—29 C.E.—Jesus was baptized, and holy spirit descended from heaven to anoint him as Messiah. Indeed, right on time in fulfillment of divine prophecy!—Luke 3:21, 22.

[12] In those days, many of the Jews were anticipating the coming of Messiah, due no doubt in part to their knowing about the "seventy weeks." (Luke 3:15; John 1:19, 20) But because of having hard hearts, the majority missed the point of the prophecy. (Matthew 15:7-9) However, we today can be strengthened in our faith by paying attention to all such features of "the prophetic word." (2 Peter 1:19-21) Not only does that "word" clearly identify Messiah, as explained in the chart on page 67; it also points us to marvelous blessings to be enjoyed under the kingdom of "Messiah the Leader."—Isaiah 9:6, 7.

MESSIAH THE KING "CUT OFF"

[13] Did the appearance of "Messiah the Leader" result in an immediate deliverance for the Jews? They expected him to be a mighty warrior, a potentate who would deliver them from harsh bondage to the Roman Empire. (John 6:14, 15) However,

12. (a) What were many of the Jews then expecting? (b) Why did they miss the point of the prophecy? (c) But how may we be benefited?

13, 14. How was Messiah's appearance and course far different from the Jews' expectations?

his Father, Jehovah, purposed a different kind of deliverance.

[14] In the prophecy of the "seventy weeks," Gabriel made it clear that, rather than the Messiah's becoming a great political ruler, he was to be "cut off, with nothing for himself." He was to die a shameful death without name or material wealth to leave for posterity. How striking the fulfillment! When Jesus was stripped for execution, the soldiers even cast lots for all that had remained to him—his outer garments.—Daniel 9:26a; Matthew 27:35.

[15] When did this execution take place? Gabriel said it would be "at the half of the [final] week" of years, that is, in the spring of 33 C.E., three and a half years after Jesus' baptism and anointing. In proof of the accuracy of the prophecy, John's Gospel indicates that Jesus was then attending the fourth Passover following his baptism.—Daniel 9:27b; John 2:13; 5:1; 6:4; 13:1.

[16] Yes, "Messiah the Leader" was "cut off." How tragic it was that the Jews did not recognize their king! But more was to come. Jerusalem must again be devastated. As Daniel's prophecy foretold:

"The city and the holy place the people of a leader that is coming will bring to their ruin. And the end of it will be by the flood. And until the end there will be war; what is decided upon is desolations."—Daniel 9:26b.

[17] True to the prophecy, the period following Messiah's 'cutting off' was marked by war "until

---

15. (a) When was Messiah "cut off"? (b) How is the accuracy of this time feature confirmed?
16, 17. (a) How were the further words of Daniel 9:26 tragically fulfilled? (b) How were Messiah's true followers of that time an example to us?

the end." Finally, in 70 C.E., the Roman army swept like a flood into beleaguered Jerusalem. The city and its temple were demolished, 'brought to their ruin.' According to the historian Josephus, 1,100,000 Jews perished in that holocaust. Happily, by that time Messiah's true followers had heeded the warning "sign" and had fled to safety in the mountains beyond the Jordan. (Matthew 24:3-16) This emphasizes also for us today how vital it is that we give attention to God's prophetic "sign" before the Kingdom 'comes' to execute judgment on the present wicked world system.—Luke 21:34-36.

MESSIAH BRINGS BENEFITS

[18] What, then, would be accomplished by Messiah's first coming? Gabriel had told Daniel:

> ***"There are seventy weeks that have been determined upon your people and upon your holy city, in order to terminate the transgression, and to finish off sin, and to make atonement for error, and to bring in righteousness for times indefinite." (Daniel 9:24a)***

Before and through his death "Messiah the Leader" would accomplish all of this! This would be not a political deliverance but a marvelous spiritual one. Through the ransoming power of his perfect human life, given in sacrifice, Jesus would remove the stain of sin and transgression from those who would accept him as Messiah, and bring them into "a new covenant" as the spiritual "Israel of God." —Galatians 6:16; Jeremiah 31:31, 33, 34.

[19] So what the Law covenant mediated by Moses had been unable to do, on the basis of its animal

---

18. What of benefit was accomplished at Messiah's first coming?
19. How did Messiah "cause sacrifice and gift offering to cease"?

sacrifices, the new covenant mediated by Messiah would now accomplish, on the basis of his one perfect human sacrifice, made "at the half of the week." Thus he would "cause sacrifice and gift offering to cease," in that the offerings of the Law would no longer be of any value. (Daniel 9:27) As the apostle Paul stated later: "The old things passed away, look! new things have come into existence. But all things are from God, who reconciled us to himself through Christ and gave us the ministry of the reconciliation."—2 Corinthians 5:17, 18.

[20] In due course, the benefits of Jesus' ransom sacrifice would extend far beyond the spiritual Israel of which Paul became a part, for he goes on to say that, by means of Christ, God reconciles "a world to himself, not reckoning to them their trespasses." (2 Corinthians 5:19) As a part of the world of mankind, are you not happy that your trespasses due to human imperfection may be forgiven on the basis of the sacrifice of the One who reconciles you to God?

[21] However, not only would the 'seventieth week' "bring in righteousness for times indefinite." Also, it would "imprint a seal upon vision and prophet." As Revelation 19:10 states, "the bearing witness to Jesus is what inspires prophesying." And Jesus, at his first coming as Messiah, literally fulfilled hundreds of prophetic utterances in what he did and what he said. This was like the implanting of an indelible seal on those prophecies, showing them to be true, accurate and having as their source the

---

20. You may be happy about what prospect for mankind?
21, 22. (a) How did the 70th week "imprint a seal upon vision and prophet"? (Daniel 9:24) (b) How was "the Holy of Holies" anointed?

Sovereign Lord Jehovah. Now, by means of the Messiah, all of God's promises of blessing for his people would be accomplished. "For no matter how many the promises of God are, they have become Yes by means of him"—the Messiah, Jesus.—Daniel 9:24b; 2 Corinthians 1:20.

[22] Also to be accomplished during that 'seventieth week' was the anointing of "the Holy of Holies." No longer could the "holy place made with hands," in Jerusalem's temple, serve God's purpose in connection with the forgiveness of sins. It had been only a copy of the reality in the great spiritual temple arrangement that came into existence with Messiah's anointing in 29 C.E. There, following his death and resurrection, Christ entered heaven to present "once for all time" the value of his human sacrifice before God's Person. (Hebrews 9:23-26) God's heavenly abode had thus taken on a new aspect. It had been anointed as "the Holy of Holies," becoming the spiritual reality typified by the Most Holy of the temple at Jerusalem. So, starting from the day of Pentecost, 33 C.E., and through to the end of the 'seventieth week,' those Jews who accepted God's provision had a unique privilege. On the basis of Christ's sacrifice presented in that "Holy of Holies," they, too, were anointed to serve as underpriests at God's spiritual temple.

[23] With regard to such Jews who would be brought into spiritual Israel, the prophecy says: "He must keep the covenant in force for the many for one week." This is the 'week of years' of 29-36 C.E., during which natural Jews were especially favored

---

23. (a) How were the Jews especially favored during the 70th week? (b) How were others favored after the "seventy weeks" ended?

in being adopted as part of the spiritual 'seed of Abraham.' (Daniel 9:27a) But then, with Peter's preaching to the uncircumcised Gentile Cornelius, the way opened up for uncircumcised people of the nations also to be brought into the Abrahamic covenant. Concerning this, Paul writes: "You are all, in fact, sons of God through your faith in Christ Jesus. For all of you who were baptized into Christ have put on Christ. There is neither Jew nor Greek, there is neither slave nor freeman, there is neither male nor female; for you are all one person in union with Christ Jesus. Moreover, if you belong to Christ, you are really Abraham's seed, heirs with reference to a promise."—Galatians 3:26-29; Acts 10:30-35, 44-48.

[24] However, what of the rest of mankind—the billions who have not been gathered to become part of the "little flock" with an inheritance in the heavens? Ah, the Abrahamic promise carries a wonderful assurance for these, too, in that God states therein: "By means of [Abraham's] seed all nations of the earth will certainly bless themselves." (Genesis 22:18) Is it your desire to share in that blessing? You may, and to this end you should pray for 'God's kingdom to come.' Also, as you keep on investigating God's Word, you will learn how you may "disown" yourself in dedication to God and follow Messiah the Leader "continually." —Luke 9:23.

---

24. (a) What wonderful assurance does the Abrahamic promise carry for still others? (b) As indicated by Luke 9:23, how may you share?

PROPHECIES FULFILLED WITH REGARD TO "MESSIAH THE LEADER" TOWARD END OF "SEVENTY WEEKS"

PROPHECY	SUBSTANCE THEREOF	FULFILLMENT
Isaiah 40:3	John the Baptizer prepares way	Matthew 3:1-3
Micah 5:2	Jesus born in Bethlehem	Matthew 2:1-6
Genesis 49:10	Out of tribe of Judah	Luke 3:23-33
Isaiah 7:14	Of a virgin	Matthew 1:23-25
Isaiah 9:7	Descendant, heir of David	Matthew 1:1, 6-17
Jeremiah 31:15	Babes killed after birth	Matthew 2:16-18
Hosea 11:1	Called out of Egypt (refuge)	Matthew 2:14, 15
Daniel 9:25	Appears at end of 69 "weeks"	Luke 3:1, 21, 22
Psalm 40:7, 8	Presents self to do God's will	Matthew 3:13-15
Isaiah 61:1, 2	Spirit anointed to preach	Luke 4:16-21
Psalm 2:7	Jehovah declares Jesus "Son"	Matthew 3:17
Isaiah 9:1, 2	Light in region of Galilee	Matthew 4:13-16
Psalm 40:9	Boldly preaches "good news"	Matthew 4:17, 23
Psalm 69:9	Zealous for Jehovah's house	John 2:13-17
Isaiah 53:1, 2	Jews do not put faith in him	John 12:37, 38
Psalm 78:2	Speaks in illustrations	Matthew 13:34, 35
Zechariah 9:9	Enters city on colt of ass	Matthew 21:1-9
Psalm 69:4	Hated without a cause	John 15:24, 25
Isaiah 42:1-4	Hope of nations; no wrangling	Matthew 12:14-21
Psalm 41:9	Unfaithful apostle betrays	John 13:18, 21-30
Zechariah 11:12	For 30 pieces of silver	Matthew 26:14-16
Psalm 2:1, 2	Rulers act against anointed	Matthew 27:1, 2
Psalm 118:22	Rejected, but sure foundation	Matthew 21:42, 43
Isaiah 8:14, 15	Becomes stone of stumbling	Luke 20:18
Psalm 27:12	False witnesses against him	Matthew 26:59-61
Isaiah 53:7	Silent before his accusers	Matthew 27:11-14
Psalm 22:16	Impaled by hands and feet	John 20:25
Isaiah 53:12	Counted with transgressors	Luke 22:36, 37
Psalm 22:7, 8	Is reviled while on stake	Matthew 27:39-43
Psalm 69:21	Given wine drugged with myrrh	Mark 15:23, 36
Zechariah 12:10	Pierced while on stake	John 19:34
Psalm 22:18	Lots cast for his garments	Matthew 27:35
Psalm 34:20	None of his bones broken	John 19:33, 36
Psalm 22:1	Forsaken to enemies by God	Matthew 27:46
Daniel 9:26, 27	Cut off after 3½ years*	John 19:14-16
Zechariah 13:7	Shepherd struck, flock scattered	Matthew 26:31, 56
Jeremiah 31:31	New covenant, sins removed	Luke 22:20
Isaiah 53:11	Bears the errors of many	Matthew 20:28
Isaiah 53:4	Carries sicknesses of mankind	Matthew 8:16, 17
Isaiah 53:9	Burial place with the rich	Matthew 27:57-60
Psalm 16:10	Raised before corruption	Acts 2:24, 27
Jonah 1:17	Resurrected on third day	Matthew 12:40
Psalm 110:1	Exalted to God's right hand	Acts 7:56

* See pages 61, 62 herein.

CHAPTER 8

'THE KINGDOM HAS DRAWN NEAR'

LET us examine in more detail the activity of "Messiah the Leader" at his first coming. The startling announcement was heard first from the lips of John the Baptizer: "Repent, for the kingdom of the heavens has drawn near." (Matthew 3:2) The future King was about to appear! As the 'seventieth week,' a "week" of special favor, approached, it was indeed high time for the Jews to repent of their sins against the righteous body of law given to them by their God, Jehovah. For now Israel was about to enter a day of judgment. Hence, John went on to say to the nation's hypocritical religious leaders: "You offspring of vipers, who has intimated to you to flee from the coming wrath? So then produce fruit that befits repentance. Already the ax is lying at the root of the trees; every tree, then, that does not produce fine fruit is to be cut down and thrown into the fire."—Matthew 3:7, 8, 10.

[2] Then it was that Jesus came from Galilee to the Jordan and asked John to baptize him. John knew that Jesus was without sin, and at first he

---

1. Why were John's words at Matthew 3:1-10 timely?
2. (a) How was Jesus' baptism different? (b) As he "commenced his work," with what did he have to contend?

refused. However, Jesus' baptism was to be different. It would symbolize his presentation of himself to Jehovah for the special work his Father had for him to do on earth. Appropriately, then, Jesus was baptized in water.

"And, as he was praying, the heaven was opened up and the holy spirit in bodily shape like a dove came down upon him, and a voice came out of heaven: 'You are my Son, the beloved; I have approved you.' Furthermore, Jesus himself, when he commenced his work, was about thirty years old."

Immediately, as Messiah and King-designate, he became the object of attacks by that old Serpent, the Devil, and those Jewish religious leaders who hypocritically professed to serve God.—Luke 3:21-23.

[3] "Now Jesus, full of holy spirit, turned away from the Jordan, and he was led about by the spirit in the wilderness for forty days, while being tempted by the Devil." (Luke 4:1, 2) Satan recognized Jesus as the "Seed" of God's promise who would in due time crush the Devil and his wicked "seed." Could Satan thwart Jehovah's purpose by causing Jesus to disobey Him? Jesus had been fasting for 40 days. So the Devil invited the hungry Jesus to turn some stones of that barren wilderness into loaves of bread. Jesus now had the power to work miracles, but, rightly, he quoted Jehovah's righteous law, saying:

"It is written, 'Man must live, not on bread alone, but on every utterance coming forth through Jehovah's mouth.'" (Matthew 4:1-4; Deuteronomy 8:3)

How unlike Eve and her husband, Adam, who had disobeyed in eating the forbidden fruit though sur-

3. How did Jesus' course when under temptation differ from that of Adam and Eve?

rounded by an abundance of other sustaining foods!

[4] Jesus' humility and complete dependence on his Father were demonstrated in the way that he met the next temptation. Satan tried to have Jesus think that he, as the Son of God, was someone important —a celebrity. Yes, let him needlessly throw himself down from the battlement of the temple, and God's angels would surely catch him so that he would come to no harm. But Jesus rejected such a foolish suggestion, quoting again from Jehovah's law, and saying:

> ***"Again it is written, 'You must not put Jehovah your God to the test.'" (Matthew 4:5-7; Deuteronomy 6:16)***

Herein lies a lesson for all who claim to be God's servants down to this day: Let no one ever presume upon his standing with Jehovah. Our being blessed by God depends not on past service or position but on our continuing to obey him in all humility, having deep respect for his arrangements and requirements.—Philippians 2:5-7.

[5] Now, the final and climactic temptation on this occasion! Oh, if Satan could only trip Jesus on the paramount issue, that of the Kingdom! So "the Devil took him along to an unusually high mountain, and showed him all the kingdoms of the world and their glory, and he said to him: 'All these things I will give you if you fall down and do an act of worship to me.'" By this simple compromise, Satan argued, Jesus could get control of the entire world

---

4. What lesson may we learn from the way that Jesus met the second temptation?
5. (a) On what paramount issue did the third temptation focus? (b) How did Jesus again use God's law in response? (c) How is this a splendid example for us today?

of mankind then and there, without having to wait through the centuries until Jehovah's due time. But again Jesus referred to Jehovah's law, as he replied:

> ***"Go away, Satan! For it is written, 'It is Jehovah your God you must worship, and it is to him alone you must render sacred service.' " (Matthew 4:8-10; Deuteronomy 6:13)***

Again, a splendid example for those who serve Jehovah today! No matter how long the road may seem to extend, let those who are rendering sacred service to Jehovah never, never cease to place God's kingdom first in their lives. May they never turn aside to build their own little "kingdoms" in the materialistic society of Satan's world.

"NO PART OF THIS WORLD"

[6] What followed Jesus' turning back the temptations of the Devil? The Bible record tells us:

> ***"Jesus commenced preaching and saying: 'Repent, you people, for the kingdom of the heavens has drawn near.' "***

In what way had the Kingdom drawn near? In that the one anointed to be King, Jesus Christ himself, was now present, "teaching . . . and preaching the good news of the kingdom." Great crowds of people followed him from place to place. (Matthew 4:17, 23-25) Jesus made it very plain that those who accepted his teaching were to be 'no part of the world, just as he was no part of the world.' They must separate themselves from the world and its violent, immoral ways. All who want to follow Jesus today must do likewise.—John 17:14, 16; 1 Peter 2:21; see also Matthew 5:27, 28; 26:52.

---

6. (a) In what way did the Kingdom now draw near? (b) In applying 1 Peter 2:21, what example of Jesus must Christians follow?

[7] With regard to false worship, Jesus told the religious leaders of his day: "You are from your father the Devil, and you wish to do the desires of your father. That one was a manslayer when he began, and he did not stand fast in the truth, because truth is not in him. When he speaks the lie, he speaks according to his own disposition, because he is a liar and the father of the lie." (John 8:44) It was most important back there for the common people to free themselves from false traditions (later incorporated into the Talmud) that had developed in the Jews' religion. And today, for those who, like the Jews, have lived all their life in the religion of their forefathers, it is vital that they examine whether or not their religious leaders have 'shoved aside' the word of God in order to teach mere human tradition.—Mark 7:9-13.

[8] When on trial for his life, Jesus declared concerning the political governments of his time:

"My kingdom is no part of this world. If my kingdom were part of this world, my attendants would have fought that I should not be delivered up to the Jews. But, as it is, my kingdom is not from this source."

The source of Jesus' kingdom was heavenly. It derived its authority from the Supreme Sovereign, Jehovah God, and not from Satan. Accordingly, Satan used his earthly "seed" to persecute Jesus and his followers.—John 18:36.

[9] Jesus therefore told his true disciples: "These

---

7. In view of Jesus' words at John 8:44, why is it vital that we today examine the teachings of religious leaders in relation to the Bible?

8, 9. (a) Why did Jesus state that his kingdom "is no part of this world"? (b) Why, then, do true Christians meet up with persecution? (c) Why should they be of good courage?

things I command you, that you love one another. If the world hates you, you know that it has hated me before it hated you. If you were part of the world, the world would be fond of what is its own. Now because you are no part of the world, but I have chosen you out of the world, on this account the world hates you." (John 15:17-19) Worshipers of Jehovah experience bitter hatred and persecution down to this present day because they separate themselves from the corrupt politics and violence that are so prevalent today. But a rich reward awaits all who finally overcome the world. As Jesus assured his disciples: "In the world you are having tribulation, but take courage! I have conquered the world."—John 16:33.

KINGLY QUALIFICATIONS

[10] What qualities would you look for in a world ruler? Most rulers of history have been "strong men," arrogant, puffed up with pride. They have usually placed personal advancement ahead of the needs of the common people. Some have boasted of building great empires, but in time all their mighty empires have collapsed, in proof of the truthfulness of King Solomon's words: "Unless Jehovah himself builds the house, it is to no avail that its builders have worked hard on it." (Psalm 127:1) These "kings" have demonstrated in fact that they do not rule by divine right. Their sovereignty has not been from Jehovah God.

[11] However, God's anointed King, Jesus Christ, is prophetically described as riding forth against his enemies "in the cause of truth and humility and

---

10, 11. (a) What shows that world rulers do not rule by divine right? (b) In contrast, how has Jesus shown himself to be qualified for kingship?

righteousness." It is said of him: "You have loved righteousness and you hate wickedness. That is why God, your God, has anointed you with the oil of exultation more than your partners"—the kings of David's line who preceded him. (Psalm 45:4, 7) In his hatred of everything that dishonors Jehovah's holy name and violates God's righteous principles, the heavenly King will in due course cleanse this earth of all wickedness, preparatory to bringing in a reign of righteousness. Has Jesus shown himself qualified to be such a ruler? Most certainly he has!

[12] When he was a perfect man, Jesus was exemplary in displaying love for God and neighbor. As a member of God's nation of Israel, dedicated to Jehovah, Jesus set the example in obeying the two greatest commandments. He said: "The first [commandment] is, 'Hear, O Israel, Jehovah our God is one Jehovah, and you must love Jehovah your God with your whole heart and with your whole soul and with your whole mind and with your whole strength.' The second is this: 'You must love your neighbor as yourself.' " (Mark 12:29-31; Deuteronomy 6:4, 5) Jesus gave of himself unsparingly in his service to Jehovah and in teaching his neighbor Jews. When these tried to detain him so as to hear more, he told them:

"Also to other cities I must declare the good news of the kingdom of God, because for this I was sent forth." (Luke 4:43)

In rendering sacred service Jesus was a worker, setting the pattern for all true Christians to follow. —Compare John 5:17.

---

12. What pattern of sacred service did Jesus set for us?

[13] Jesus showed himself to be loving and compassionate. In his heart, he yearned to see his people relieved of the heavy burdens imposed on them by their religious oppressors. So he told them about the Kingdom, and sent out his disciples, saying:

"As you go, preach, saying, 'The kingdom of the heavens has drawn near.' "—Matthew 9:35–10:7.

[14] This King-designate invited the people, saying: "Come to me, all you who are toiling and loaded down, and I will refresh you. Take my yoke upon you and become my disciples, for I am mild-tempered and lowly in heart, and you will find refreshment for your souls. For my yoke is kindly and my load is light." (Matthew 11:28-30) Jesus, as God's heavenly King over all mankind, will show that same kind of compassion, and he will see to it, as he did while on earth, that his Kingdom associates are organized to provide the relief and kindly oversight that humans really need. All who live on earth under Jesus' Kingdom rule will indeed find refreshment for their souls.

FLAWLESS IN INTEGRITY

[15] Above all, mankind's future King demonstrated flawless integrity and obedience to his heavenly Father, down to a cruel death on a torture stake. As that hour of execution drew near, Jesus prayed to Jehovah, saying, "Father, glorify your name." Jehovah's voice responded out of heaven: "I both glorified it and will glorify it again." In sanctifying his Father's name, Jesus gave the complete answer

---

13, 14. (a) How did Jesus regard people? (b) Why did he go out preaching, and why did he send forth others? (c) What kind of oversight may humans expect under the Kingdom?
15. How did Jesus give the complete answer to Satan's challenge?

to Satan's challenge. He demonstrated that a perfect man could prove faithful to God under every kind of trial that the adversary might bring against him. So Jesus could say: "Now there is a judging of this world; now the ruler of this world [Satan] will be cast out"—completely discredited, proved to be a liar. The Jewish religious leaders, as the 'seed of the serpent,' would cause a painful "heel" wound to be inflicted on the "seed" of God's womanlike organization, but God would resurrect his worthy Son to spirit life.—Genesis 3:15; John 12:27-31.

[16] Jesus' love of righteousness, his hatred of lawlessness, his deep fondness for mankind and, above all, his unswerving obedience in doing his Father's will to the glory of Jehovah's name—all these things prove this loyal Son to be admirably qualified as earth's future King. Would you not like to enter into eternal life as the happy subject of such a king?

[17] No matter how good or how bad your way of life has been until now, you may realize that hope of everlasting life on an earth made glorious. Why, even the repentant thief that was executed with Jesus was given such a resurrection hope! For when he said to Jesus, "Remember me when you get into your kingdom," Jesus replied: "Truly I tell you today, You will be with me in Paradise." (Luke 23:42, 43) Soon, Paradise is to become a reality. Are you, too, prayerfully reaching out for the 'coming' of the Kingdom and its blessings?

16, 17. (a) Why may we have strong confidence in earth's future King? (b) How do the Scriptures indicate the hope of a paradise earth to be a real one? (c) Should your previous way of life hinder you in reaching out for that hope?

THE GREATEST MAN EVER ON EARTH
As King-designate, he proved
integrity to the death, and
by his shed blood ransomed
mankind from sin and death

CHAPTER 9

KINGDOM HEIRS KEEP INTEGRITY

PROVING faithful to the death, Jesus inherited a name more excellent than that of the angels. Of all God's intelligent creatures, he was *the One* to demonstrate that a son of God could keep perfect integrity to God, thus showing Satan to be a liar. Accordingly, the apostle Paul writes: "After he had made a purification for our sins [by providing the ransom] he sat down on the right hand of the Majesty in lofty places." What a grand example he set for all who await the 'coming' of the Kingdom—both those of the "little flock" who inherit the heavenly kingdom and those who will be the earthly subjects of that kingdom! As the same apostle states later: "Let us run with endurance the race that is set before us, as we look intently at the Chief Agent and Perfecter of our faith, Jesus. For the joy that was set before him he endured a torture stake, despising shame, and has sat down at the right hand of the throne of God." —Hebrews 1:3, 4; 12:1, 2.

---

1. (a) Why did Jesus inherit a more excellent name? (b) Who may profit by his example, and how?

[2] Not only did Jesus provide a splendid example for his followers, but he also taught and trained them, in order that they could continue God's work after he had gone away.

"He went journeying from city to city and from village to village, preaching and declaring the good news of the kingdom of God. And the twelve were with him."—Luke 8:1.

[3] Later, Jesus sent the 12 out on their own "to preach the kingdom of God and to heal." "They went through the territory from village to village, declaring the good news and performing cures everywhere." (Luke 9:2, 6) In the cities and villages they were to search out deserving ones, and this they did by going to the people's homes. It required courageous maintaining of integrity on their part, even as it does of Jehovah's Witnesses in many territories today, because of opposition to the message. Jesus said: "If the house is deserving, let the peace you wish it come upon it; but if it is not deserving, let the peace from you return upon you. Wherever anyone does not take you in or listen to your words, on going out of that house or that city shake the dust off your feet."—Matthew 10:7, 11-14.

[4] Later, when Jesus designated 70 other disciples, he told them: "Look! I am sending you forth as lambs in among wolves." These, too, were to visit the homes of the people, for Jesus went on to say: "Wherever you enter into a house say first, 'May this house have peace.' And if a friend of peace is there, your peace will rest upon him. But if there is not, it will turn back to you." Even if the people

---

2-4. (a) How did Jesus progressively train and organize his disciples for preaching activity? (b) How do we know that they took the "good news" to the people's homes? (c) What fine precedent did this activity provide for God's servants today?

did not listen to the "good news," they were to be warned that the kingdom of God had come near! (Luke 10:3-11) This provides a fine precedent for the work of Jehovah's Witnesses today, as these go from house to house with God's message of comfort and of warning.—Isaiah 61:1, 2.

PREACHING DESPITE PERSECUTIONS

5 At Jesus' death, those disciples were scattered. But on numerous occasions following his resurrection in the spirit he appeared to them in materialized bodies, to reassure and strengthen them. (1 Corinthians 15:3-8) On one of these occasions Jesus asked Peter three times whether he really loved and had affection for him. Peter became grieved at this, but three times Jesus emphasized that, in evidence of love and affection, Peter must feed and shepherd his "lambs," his "little sheep." (John 21:15-17) At another appearance, Jesus told his 11 faithful disciples:

> ***"All authority has been given me in heaven and on the earth. Go therefore and make disciples of people of all the nations, baptizing them in the name of the Father and of the Son and of the holy spirit, teaching them to observe all the things I have commanded you. And, look! I am with you all the days until the conclusion of the system of things." (Matthew 28:18-20)***

There was much work ahead for them.

6 Jesus had told his disciples: "Most truly I say to you, He that exercises faith in me, that one also will do the works that I do; and he will do works greater than these, because I am going my way to

---

5. In what ways did the resurrected Jesus emphasize the kind of work ahead for his followers?
6. Why would Jesus' disciples do 'greater works'?

the Father." (John 14:12) They would cover a larger territory than he had and would carry on the work of preaching God's kingdom over a much longer period of time.

[7] After arriving at the right hand of his Father in heaven, Jesus did a marvelous thing. On the day of Pentecost, 33 C.E., he poured out holy spirit upon his waiting disciples, anointing them to be heirs with him of God's heavenly kingdom. Eventually, 144,000 would be chosen from mankind to be kings and priests in heaven with Christ. As a result of the thorough witness given on just that one day, 3,000 Jews and proselytes heartily embraced the word and were baptized.—John 14:2, 3; Revelation 14:1-5; 20:4, 6; Acts 2:1-4, 14, 40, 41.

[8] The preaching of the "good news" spread through the territory of Jerusalem like wildfire. And so did opposition to God's kingdom. Soon the apostles were hauled before the Jewish court of the Sanhedrin and forbidden to speak in the name of Jesus. Would they hold fast their integrity? Peter and John replied: "Whether it is righteous in the sight of God to listen to you rather than to God, judge for yourselves. But as for us, we cannot stop speaking about the things we have seen and heard." On this occasion the apostles were released, and they and their companions immediately gave thanks to God, petitioning him: "Now, Jehovah, . . . grant your slaves to keep speaking your word with all

---

7. What marvelous thing led to a thorough witness on the day of Pentecost, and with what astounding result?

8-11. (a) What conflict now raged between the Jews' leaders and the apostles? (b) How did the apostles show themselves to be integrity-keepers? (c) According to Acts 5:40-42, what fine example did those apostles leave for God's servants today?

boldness." So they continued to preach with the help of Jehovah's spirit.—Acts 4:19, 20, 29, 31.

[9] Again the religious leaders arrested the apostles and put them in jail. But it was not God's will that they stay there. During the night Jehovah's angel released them, so that daybreak found them teaching again in Jerusalem's temple.—Acts 5:17-21.

[10] What could the Sanhedrin do to stop the spread of the "good news"? Once more, the apostles were brought into court, and the high priest charged them: "We positively ordered you not to keep teaching upon the basis of [Jesus'] name, and yet, look! you have filled Jerusalem with your teaching, and you are determined to bring the blood of this man upon us." The uncompromising response of those apostles rings out, down through 19 centuries:

"We must obey God as ruler rather than men"!

What could the Jews do with these integrity-keepers? The law teacher Gamaliel gave wise advice: "Do not meddle with these men, but let them alone; (because, if this scheme and this work is from men, it will be overthrown; but if it is from God, you will not be able to overthrow them;) otherwise, you may perhaps be found fighters actually against God."—Acts 5:27-39.

[11] So the apostles were flogged, ordered to stop speaking and then were released. What was their reaction? They rejoiced in that they were counted worthy to suffer on the basis of Jesus' name.

"And every day in the temple and from house to house they continued without letup teaching and declaring the good news about the Christ, Jesus." (Acts 5:40-42)

These Kingdom heirs were determined to endure

what was necessary in order to continue doing God's work. They thus set a fine example for all witnesses of the true God who have continued proclaiming the Kingdom "publicly and from house to house" down to this day.—Acts 20:20, 21.

THE KINGDOM "GOOD NEWS" SPREADS

[12] Again the persecution intensified, so that all except the apostles were scattered into nearby Judea and Samaria. But this served only to expand the witness, for "those who had been scattered went through the land declaring the good news of the word." (Acts 8:1-4) Interestingly, the same thing has happened in modern times. When dictatorial governments have tried to stop Jehovah's Witnesses by scattering them to isolated areas, they have kept on preaching there, and the "good news" has spread.

[13] However, back there in the first century, was the Kingdom message going to be carried only to the Jews and the neighboring Samaritans? Would the complete membership of the kingdom of the heavens be made up from among them only? Even with the marvelous witness that was being given, that was not to be. Apparently in 36 C.E., as God's special "week" of favor toward the Jews ended, Jehovah directed Peter to visit an Italian army officer, Cornelius, at his home in Caesarea. As Peter was preaching to this non-Jew and his household, holy spirit fell upon them, anointing them to be Kingdom heirs. They were baptized as the first un-

---

12. As shown at Acts 8:1-4, how does persecution often result in the further spreading of the "good news"?

13, 14. (a) When did God's special week of favor toward the Jews end, and who then were admitted as Kingdom heirs? (b) How do Paul's words at Acts 13 and Romans 11 bear this out?

circumcised Gentile converts to Christianity.—Acts 10:1-48.

[14] Later, when the apostle Paul and his companions met with violent opposition from the Jews in Antioch of Pisidia, Paul told those Jews: "It was necessary for the word of God to be spoken first to you. Since you are thrusting it away from you and do not judge yourselves worthy of everlasting life, look! we turn to the nations. In fact, Jehovah has laid commandment upon us in these words, 'I have appointed you as a light of nations, for you to be a salvation to the extremity of the earth.'" (Acts 13:46, 47) As Paul stated later in an illustration, those unbelieving Jews were like natural branches lopped off an olive tree. The Jews could have provided the full number of Kingdom heirs. However, in their place, "people of the nations," like branches of a wild olive tree, were being grafted in, and thus "all [spiritual] Israel," up to its full Kingdom membership, would be "saved."—Romans 11:13-26; Galatians 6:16.

INTEGRITY UNDER "TRIBULATIONS"

[15] Despite further persecutions, that faithful traveling overseer, the apostle Paul, returned to Antioch, in order to strengthen and encourage the disciples and to build up the congregational organization. It was then that Paul said:

"We must enter into the kingdom of God through many tribulations."—Acts 14:21-23.

[16] Paul continued to have his share of hardships

15, 16. (a) What did Paul do and say with regard to "tribulations," and what fine pattern does this provide us? (b) What should be our attitude toward opposition by governments or family members, and what outcome are we promised?

and trials. But he was exemplary in holding fast his integrity. He provided a fine pattern for many in modern times who have to put up a hard fight for the faith. Some of these have had to contend with beatings, imprisonments and danger to life itself. Opposition has come from dictatorial governments, or even from dearly loved relatives. Some have been disowned by family members on account of their accepting and acting on "this good news of the kingdom." (Matthew 24:14) However, such ones have been greatly comforted by Jesus' words: "No one has left house or brothers or sisters or mother or father or children or fields for my sake and for the sake of the good news who will not get a hundredfold now in this period of time, houses and brothers and sisters and mothers and children and fields, with persecutions, and in the coming system of things everlasting life." (Mark 10:29, 30) They do indeed reap "a hundredfold" in their intimate relationship with Jehovah and his Son and in their joyful association with Jehovah's earth-wide family.

[17] The apostle Paul and his companions had to fight also against the world's temptations to immorality and materialism. They were just human, as we are. When faced with such enticements we should do as did Paul, who said: "I pummel my body and lead it as a slave, that, after I have preached to others, I myself should not become disapproved somehow." And like Paul, we, too, may find protection in telling our neighbors about God's kingdom. As Paul said concerning such sacred ser-

---

17. (a) With what temptations did early Christians also have to contend? (b) What splendid example and advice did Paul provide for us?

vice: "Really, woe is me if I did not declare the good news!"—1 Corinthians 9:16, 27.

"COMPLETELY VICTORIOUS"

[18] The apostle Paul also told fellow anointed Christians: "If, then, we are children [of God], we are also heirs: heirs indeed of God, but joint heirs with Christ, provided we suffer together that we may also be glorified together." But what he went on to say applies equally well to the "great crowd" of "other sheep," who today are reaching out for the glorious reward of life eternal in the paradise earth. (Revelation 7:9; John 10:16) Paul encourages all true Christians, saying:

"Who will separate us from the love of the Christ? Will tribulation or distress or persecution or hunger or nakedness or danger or sword? . . . To the contrary, in all these things we are coming off completely victorious through him that loved us. For I am convinced that neither death nor life nor angels nor governments nor things now here nor things to come nor powers nor height nor depth nor any other creation will be able to separate us from God's love that is in Christ Jesus our Lord." (Romans 8:17, 35-39; see also 2 Corinthians 11:22-28.)

Are you cultivating that kind of confidence in God's love and in the 'coming' of the kingdom of the Lord Jesus? You should be!

[19] Another danger against which you need to be fortified in "the last days" is false teaching. Paul warned against this also. (Acts 20:29, 30; 2 Timothy 3:1, 13) From where do false teachers come, and how may we guard against them?

---

18. What encouragement did Paul leave for all true Christians, and how do you respond thereto?
19. What warning did Paul give about another mortal danger?

CHAPTER 10

A COUNTERFEIT KINGDOM ARISES

IN THE face of the cruelest persecutions, the young Christian congregation continued to flourish and expand. The truth of the good news concerning God's kingdom by Messiah kept on "bearing fruit and increasing in all the world." As the Kingdom proclaimers penetrated into new territories opposers lamented that "these men that have overturned the inhabited earth are present here also."—Colossians 1:5, 6; Acts 17:6.

2 However, what could mere men do to stop the spread of truth? History records that in the first three centuries of our Common Era the Caesars of the Roman Empire brought some 10 different waves of persecution against the early Christians, but all to no avail. Those who followed in Jesus' steps, "solid in the faith," refused to compromise even though that "roaring lion," the Devil, saw to it that many of them were thrown to literal lions or otherwise tortured to the death.—1 Peter 5:8, 9; compare 1 Corinthians 15:32; 2 Timothy 4:17.

3 Since the frontal attack of direct persecution

---

1. To what extent did the "good news" flourish in early times?
2. What efforts did the Devil make to stop the spread of truth, but why did he fail?
3. Why must you put on the "complete suit of armor from God"?

usually failed, the Devil sought to entrap Jesus' followers by more subtle means. They were surrounded by a proud, immoral, pleasure-mad world, and Satan used this to the full in trying to turn them away from God's service. They needed to "stand firm," as the apostle Paul repeats three times at Ephesians 6:11-18, in detailing the spiritual "armor from God" that they must use. Have you yourself put on this "complete suit of armor from God"? You must have it in order to withstand the trials of these "last days." (2 Timothy 3:1-5) And Christians back there in the first century needed it. Why especially so?

[4] Theirs was a pure and simple faith. At that time all of them were spirit-anointed Christians who looked forward to a future resurrection "into the everlasting kingdom of our Lord and Savior Jesus Christ." (2 Peter 1:11; 1 Corinthians 15:50) At least from about the year 96 C.E., when the aged apostle John received the Revelation by divine inspiration, they appreciated that their number, as a "little flock," would be 144,000. As associate 'kings and priests' with the Christ in heaven, they would rule over the earth for 1,000 years. John was shown that "after" the 144,000 of spiritual Israel had been gathered, an unnumbered "great crowd" of loyal men and women, "out of all nations and tribes and peoples and tongues," would be identified. As a class these would survive the final "great tribulation" on earth to become the nucleus of the human society to enjoy millennial blessings under the Kingdom rule.—Luke 12:32; Revelation 7:4, 9-17; 20:1-6; 21:1-5.

---

4. In the first century, what basic Kingdom truths did Christians come to understand?

THE GREAT APOSTASY

[5] What, then, was the Devil's subtle mode of attack? Referring back to faithless Israel, the apostle Peter had warned: "There also came to be false prophets among the people, as there will also be false teachers among you. These very ones will quietly bring in destructive sects . . . Also, with covetousness they will exploit you with counterfeit words." (2 Peter 2:1, 3) These false sectarian teachers, with their counterfeit religious doctrines, had already begun to appear by the end of the first century, for it was about the year 98 C.E. that the apostle John wrote: "Just as you have heard that antichrist is coming, even now there have come to be many antichrists . . . They went out from us, but they were not of our sort."—1 John 2:18, 19.

[6] As early as 51 C.E., in what appears to have been his second canonical letter, the apostle Paul had warned concerning false teachings about the "day of Jehovah." He wrote: "Let no one seduce you in any manner, because it will not come unless the apostasy comes first and the man of lawlessness gets revealed, the son of destruction." Who could this "man of lawlessness" be? It must refer to apostate religious leaders who are lawless in that, while they claim to be Christians, they "do not know God" and "do not obey the good news about our Lord Jesus." (2 Thessalonians 1:6-8; 2:1-3) How could such an apostate class arise in the Christian congregation?

[7] While the apostles of Jesus Christ were still alive,

5, 6. (a) What scriptures show that, even then, the Devil was using a more subtle mode of attack? (b) In a word, what was it?
7. How were some of Jesus' followers ensnared, with what result?

they acted as a restraint against the intrusion of false teaching, but "the mystery of this lawlessness" was already at work, "according to the operation of Satan," and it came to the fore in the second century. Whereas Jesus had stated of his followers, "all you are brothers," a desire for personal prominence caused some to be ensnared by the Devil. They now made a distinction between clergy and laity. Gradually the situation prophesied by the apostle Paul arose: "There will be a period of time when they will not put up with the healthful teaching, but, in accord with their own desires, they will accumulate teachers for themselves to have their ears tickled; and they will turn their ears away from the truth."—2 Timothy 4:3, 4; 2 Thessalonians 2:6-10; Matthew 23:8.

[8] Where, then, did they turn their ears? To doctrines that emanated from the cradle of false religion in ancient Babylon, and to the philosophies of the Greeks, which were so popular in the Roman world of that time. As *M'Clintock and Strong's Cyclopaedia* comments: "The simplicity of the Gospel was corrupted; pompous rites and ceremonies were introduced; worldly honors and emoluments were conferred on the teachers of Christianity, and the kingdom of Christ in a great measure converted into a kingdom of this world." And to this the *Encyclopaedia Britannica* adds the following: "Nothing perhaps has tended more thoroughly to corrupt Christianity than the introduction into it of superstitions which are really pagan themselves, or have been suggested by pagan practices. Paganism, unable to oppose Christianity successfully, has done

8. (a) What were the two main sources of false teaching? (b) How do encyclopedias describe the corrupting of Christianity?

much to corrupt it, and in numberless ways has made inroads into its purity."

[9] What are some of these superstitions and pagan practices? Outstanding is the teaching of the Greek philosopher Plato that the human soul is immortal. Such a belief requires that the soul must go somewhere at death, to a heaven of bliss, a purgatory for cleansing or a fiery hell for eternal torment. This flies in the face of such scriptures in the Bible as Psalm 146:4; Ecclesiastes 9:5, 10; Matthew 10:28 and Romans 6:23.

ORIGINS OF CATHOLICISM

[10] In his *Essays and Sketches*, the 19th-century Roman Catholic cardinal John Henry Newman indicates the origin of many teachings of his Church, saying: "The phenomenon, admitted on all hands, is this:—That great portion of what is generally received as Christian truth is, in its rudiments or in its separate parts, to be found in heathen philosophies and religions. For instance, the doctrine of a Trinity is found both in the East and in the West; so is the ceremony of washing; so is the rite of sacrifice. The doctrine of the Divine Word is Platonic; the doctrine of the Incarnation is Indian." Then, replying to a critic who argues, "These things are in heathenism, therefore they are not Christian," the cardinal says: "We, on the contrary, prefer to say, 'these things are in Christianity, therefore they are

---

9. (a) What common beliefs stem from the teaching that the human soul is immortal? (b) How does the Bible refute such doctrines?

10, 11. (a) What does Cardinal Newman admit as to many teachings of his Church? (b) Since he says Church practices and teachings are "of pagan origin," can these really be regarded as holy?

not heathen.'" But their source is the Babylonian and Greek teachings that existed centuries before the birth of Roman Catholicism. Moreover, they are not to be found in God's Word, the Bible.

[11] That the great apostasy went back to pagan religion for its teachings and ceremonies is further confirmed by Cardinal Newman's comments in his book *The Development of Christian Doctrine,* where he writes: "Constantine, in order to recommend the new [Roman Catholic] religion to the heathen, transferred into it the outward ornaments to which they had been accustomed in their own." Then, after listing many of the practices of his church, the cardinal admits that these "are all of pagan origin, and sanctified by their adoption into the Church." But can false teaching be "sanctified," or made holy?

[12] The cardinal here refers to Constantine the Great, Roman emperor of the fourth century. What was Constantine's interest in religion? Years after his invasion of Rome in 312 C.E., Constantine made it known that, on the eve of his conquest, he saw the vision of a flaming cross, with the motto "By This Conquer." This he inscribed on his standard. He adopted the foundations for the Roman Catholic religion apparently to gain support in furthering his own political ends, and he fused into the "Christian" religious system the pagan beliefs that were still nearest to his heart.

[13] The *Encyclopaedia Britannica* says of Constantine: "Paganism must still have been an operative

---

12, 13. (a) Under what circumstances and with what motive did Constantine interest himself in the Roman Catholic religion? (b) What shows whether Constantine had become a Christian at heart?

belief with the man who, down almost to the close of his life, retained so many pagan superstitions. . . . Constantine was entitled to be called Great in virtue rather of what he did than what he was. Tested by character, indeed, he stands among the lowest of all those to whom the epithet ["Great"] has in ancient or modern times been applied." This is demonstrated in that he stooped even to the murder of several of his own family members. His pagan title, "Pontifex Maximus," was later transferred to the popes of the Roman Catholic Church.

[14] Down through the Dark and Middle Ages, the popes of Rome ruled much like kings on earth. They did not wait for Christ to set up his millennial rule from the heavens. They wanted a "kingdom" *then*, for their own selfish advantage. The *Encyclopaedia Britannica* describes it in these words: "One of the earliest causes of the corruption of Christianity was the attempt to translate the Christian kingdom of God into a visible monarchy in which the saints inherited the earth in a literal way." It was no wonder that honest persons wanted to take issue with such "corruption of Christianity"! However, the cruel Inquisition, which by burnings at the stake alone took more than 30,000 lives, long served to keep so-called heretics in check. But not for all time!

WHAT OF PROTESTANTISM?

[15] At midday, October 31, 1517, Roman Catholic priest Martin Luther nailed 95 theses of protest

---

14. Did the popes of Rome truly represent the kingdom of God, and why do you so answer?
15. (a) What actually did the Protestant Reformation become? (b) In what way is Protestantism in bondage down to our day?

to the church door at Wittenberg, Germany. The Protestant Reformation was under way. However, rather than bring a return to pure Christian doctrine and sacred service to God, the Reformation became largely political. Territorial gains were sought through fighting religious wars, such as the 30 Years' War of 1618-1648 in Europe, in which millions of lives were lost. Many countries set up their state religions, and these continued to teach Catholicism's key doctrines, such as the immortality of the soul, a hellfire of torment, the Trinity, infant baptism and many others. They remain in bondage to these teachings of the great apostasy right down to this present day.

"BABYLON THE GREAT"

[16] The practice of false religion is not limited to persons that profess to be Christian. The prophet Jeremiah warns us:

"Flee out of the midst of Babylon, and provide escape each one for his own soul." (Jeremiah 51:6)

This has meaning for us today. Even in Jeremiah's day, Babylon was notorious for its depraved religious ritual and its multiplicity of gods. But the modern-day Babylon is international in its scope. How did this come about?

[17] Following the flood of Noah's day, it was at Babylon that wicked Nimrod, "a mighty hunter in opposition to Jehovah," started to build a city-kingdom and likely the religious tower reaching into the heavens. Jehovah thwarted those plans by confusing the tongues of mankind and scattering them "over all the surface of the earth." *But their*

16, 17. (a) What meaning does Jeremiah 51:6 have for us today? (b) How did Babylon's religion become international in scope?

false religion went with them. It was the root from which most of the world's religions have grown. —Genesis 10:8-10; 11:1-9.

[18] As we have noted, Constantine fused such false religion into Christian teachings when he laid the foundations for the Roman Catholic religion. This, in turn, became the source of much of the doctrine of Protestantism. The non-"Christian" religions of the earth also have their roots in ancient Babylon. All together, the pseudo-Christian and the non-"Christian" religions make up a world empire of false religion. It is a counterfeit kingdom that the apostle John referred to as "Babylon the Great . . . the great city that has a [religious] kingdom over the kings of the earth." (Revelation 17:5, 18) So in order to "provide escape each one for his own soul," we are well advised to flee out of the counterfeit Babylonish "kingdom," yes, flee to God's kingdom!

18. From what counterfeit kingdom must we flee, and to where?

SATAN ASSAULTS GOD'S KINGDOM SERVANTS BY—

- The direct frontal attack of persecutions—through misinformed relatives, governments, religionists
- Enticing to immorality in today's permissive society
- Fostering pride of station, wealth, race, nation
- Trying to make them lovers of pleasures rather than lovers of God—absorbed in entertainment
- Advancing atheistic, evolutionary teachings
- Misrepresenting true Christianity by means of Christendom's apostate counterfeit kingdom
- Raising up false teachers to sow doubt among true Christians and subtly discourage them

WE MAY CONQUER SATAN'S WORLD BY OUR FAITH

CHAPTER 11

KINGDOM ILLUSTRATIONS

WHILE he was with his disciples, Jesus spoke many parables, or illustrations. These show what is involved in membership in the kingdom of the heavens. They indicate what course must be taken by the "little flock" of Kingdom heirs, and also by those who will gain everlasting life on earth under that kingdom. These "other sheep," too, rejoice to know about the prophecies concerning the Kingdom, and they pray fervently for it to 'come.'—Luke 12:32; John 10:16; 1 Thessalonians 5:16-20.

[2] After he had related one of these parables to the people, Jesus' disciples came to him and asked: "Why is it you speak to them by the use of illustrations?" In reply, Jesus said:

"To you it is granted to understand the sacred secrets of the kingdom of the heavens, but to those people it is not granted." (Matthew 13:10, 11)

And why not? It was because they were not willing to dig down and get the deeper meaning of his

---

1. Why are Jesus' parables of interest to all who serve God?
2, 3. (a) Why did Jesus use illustrations? (b) Why did others besides his disciples fail to understand? (c) Unlike those described at Matthew 13:13-15, why should we diligently study God's Word?

words, so that their hearts would motivate them to action in behalf of the "good news." They did not regard the Kingdom as "treasure" or a "pearl of high value."—Matthew 13:44-46.

3 Jesus quoted the prophecy of Isaiah as having fulfillment in those unbelievers, saying: "By hearing, you will hear but by no means get the sense of it; and, looking, you will look but by no means see. For the heart of this people has grown unreceptive, and with their ears they have heard without response, and they have shut their eyes; that they might never see with their eyes and hear with their ears and get the sense of it with their hearts and turn back, and I heal them." (Matthew 13:13-15) We should want to avoid being like those unappreciative people. Let us, then, apply ourselves to the study of God's Word.

4 In his parable introduced at Matthew chapter 13:3-8, Jesus describes himself as "a sower" of seed. He sows "the word of the kingdom" in different kinds of hearts. Some persons' hearts are like roadside soil. Before the seed can take root, the Devil sends his henchmen like "birds" to pluck "the word away from their hearts in order that they may not believe and be saved." Other hearts are like rocky soil. At first, they accept the word with joy, but then the tender plant withers under trial or persecution. Some seed falls among "thorns," where it is choked out by "anxieties and riches and pleasures of this life." Ah, but there is also the "seed" sown upon the right kind of soil!

"This is the one hearing the word and getting the sense of it, who really does bear fruit and produces, this one a hun-

---

4. (a) What types of hearts fail to profit from the word? (b) How may we be blessed if we strive to get the sense of the word?

dredfold, that one sixty, the other thirty." (Matthew 13:18-23; Mark 4:3-9, 14-20; Luke 8:4-8, 11-15)

Yes, we will be blessed and our sacred service to our God will become really fruitful if we receive the word into appreciative hearts and expend ourselves in behalf of God's kingdom!

ANOTHER "SOWER"

[5] Alone of the Gospels, Mark's account follows up this parable of the "sower" with an illustration involving a different "sower." Just before giving this illustration, Jesus told his disciples in private: "Pay attention to what you are hearing." Then he tied in the parable, saying:

> ***"In this way the kingdom of God is just as when a man casts the seed upon the ground, and he sleeps at night and rises up by day, and the seed sprouts and grows tall, just how he does not know." (Mark 4:24-27)***

Obviously, this "man" is not the glorified Lord Jesus Christ, for the latter no longer needs an earthly night's sleep. Nor would it be correct to say that the Son of God, who worked with his Father in creating all things, "does not know" how growth takes place. (Colossians 1:16) So in the context we can appreciate that the "man" has reference to the individual Christian who should be 'paying attention' to matters related to "the kingdom of God."

[6] Each "sower" should watch with what personality traits he is sowing, and also the environment in which he sows. Without our being aware of it, the development of our personality may be influenced

---

5. (a) To what other illustration are we now encouraged to pay attention? (b) Why could this "man" not be the Lord Jesus?
6. What two things should each "sower" watch, and why?

for good or for bad, according to the "ground" or kind of people among whom we associate as we seek to develop Christian qualities—be that inside or outside the congregation. (Compare 1 Corinthians 15:33.) Finally, "the full grain" will appear in the head, and we will harvest accordingly. (Mark 4:28, 29) How important that those of the "little flock," and indeed all who reach out for everlasting life in God's Kingdom arrangement, watch what and where they sow with regard to the developing of Christlike personalities!—Ephesians 4:17-24; Galatians 6:7-9.

A COUNTERFEIT KINGDOM

[7] Mark's account describes Jesus as going on to say:

"With what are we to liken the kingdom of God, or in what illustration shall we set it out?" (Mark 4:30)

Then he invites us to look at the Kingdom in a different setting. Indeed, these illustrations help us to view the Kingdom from various standpoints, just as we might inspect a building on the outside and on the inside, and from a number of different angles.

[8] So to what should we liken the kingdom of God? Jesus answers:

"Like a mustard grain, which at the time it was sown in the ground was the tiniest of all the seeds that are on the earth—but when it has been sown, it comes up and becomes

---

7. How do the various parables help us to view the Kingdom?
8. (a) Why could not the phenomenal growth from the mustard grain have reference to the Kingdom heirs? (b) Why does this logically fit Christendom's "kingdom"? (c) How does God's description of apostate Israel support this view?

greater than all other vegetables and produces great branches, so that the birds of heaven are able to find lodging under its shadow." (Mark 4:30-32)

A phenomenal growth this—and surely, to something far more expansive than the "little flock" of 144,000 Kingdom heirs, to whom 'the Father has approved of giving the kingdom'! (Luke 12:32; Revelation 14:1, 3) Rather, it is the growth of the great counterfeit "tree" of Christendom as an apostasy from the congregation that Jesus had planted. (Luke 13:18, 19) It is huge! It boasts more than 900,000,000 members worldwide, for whom it claims a destiny in the heavens. This apostate kingdom was foreshadowed long ago by backsliding Israel, of which Jehovah said: "I had planted you as a choice red vine, all of it a true seed. So how have you been changed toward me into the degenerate shoots of a foreign vine?"—Jeremiah 2:21-23; see also Hosea 10:1-4.

[9] According to Matthew's description of this "tree," "the birds of heaven come and find lodging among its branches." Apparently, they are the same "birds" of the earlier parable that gobble up the "word of the kingdom" that falls by the roadside. (Matthew 13:4, 19, 31, 32) Those "birds" roost in the hundreds of sectarian branches of the "tree." They represent the apostate "man of lawlessness," the clergy of Christendom. They will lose their sheltered perch when God chops down that "tree," along with all other false religion. Stand clear, now! For the crash

---

9. (a) Who are the "birds" and the branches of the "tree"? (b) In view of the statements at 2 Thessalonians 1 and Matthew 7, why should we now stand clear of that "tree"?

of that "tree" is imminent!—Compare 2 Thessalonians 1:6-9; 2:3; Matthew 7:19-23.

[10] Appropriately, Luke presents the parable of the "mustard grain" as a follow-up to Jesus' denunciation of the apostate religionists of his day. And as if to emphasize the point, both Matthew and Luke next portray Jesus as giving the parable of the "leaven." (Matthew 13:32, 33; Luke 13:10-21) When used figuratively in the Bible, leaven always has an unfavorable connotation, as when Jesus warned his disciples to "watch out for the leaven of the Pharisees and Sadducees," and when the apostle Paul counseled Christians to clear away the "leaven of badness and wickedness."—Matthew 16:6, 11, 12; 1 Corinthians 5:6-8; Galatians 5:7-9.

[11] In the illustration, a feature in connection with "the kingdom of the heavens" is said to be like leaven that a woman hides in three measures of flour. So the whole mass of flour becomes fermented. This pictures the stealthy corrupting of the professed Christian congregation with false Babylonish teaching and practice, resulting in the massive structure of Christendom's counterfeit kingdom. This should serve as a warning for us. Viewing the sorry result of apostasy in Christendom, the "little flock" of Kingdom heirs and their companions today should beware that the "leaven" of false, deceptive teachings is never permitted to contaminate their heartfelt appreciation of the purity and truth of the "word of the kingdom."

10, 11. (a) In what contexts do Matthew and Luke present the parable of the "mustard grain," and why appropriately so? (b) What admonition and warning does the Kingdom parable of the leaven provide for us?

THE SOWER AND HIS "ENEMY"

[12] In another illustration Jesus likens "the kingdom of the heavens" to "a man that sowed fine seed in his field." Then, "while *men* were sleeping, his enemy came and oversowed weeds in among the wheat, and left." What kind of fruitage could be expected from that field? Jesus went on to identify this sower as himself, "the Son of man," the sowing of whose Kingdom seed results in fruitage of wheatlike Christians, "the sons of the kingdom." The enemy is "the Devil," and the "weeds" are "the sons of the wicked one"—his hypocritical religious "seed." (Compare Genesis 3:15.) In fulfillment, some true Christians kept growing up among the conglomeration of "weeds" that have marked the great apostasy from the first century onward. But now in our 20th century, we have come to the time for harvest—"a conclusion of a system of things, and the reapers are angels"!—Matthew 13:24-30, 36-39.

[13] At last, under angelic direction, the "wheat" is separated from the "weeds." The clear distinction between the two has been made manifest. As we shall see, the evidence abounds that "the Son of man" is today present in his heavenly kingdom, gathering wheatlike true Christians to Kingdom activity. But what of Christendom and its teachers of apostasy? Jesus' parable goes on to say:

"The Son of man will send forth his angels, and they will collect out from his kingdom all things that cause stumbling and persons who are doing lawlessness."

For centuries the clergy of Christendom have stum-

12, 13. (a) In the parable of the "wheat" and the "weeds," how does Jesus identify the principals? (b) What is the harvest, and what evidence do we see that it is taking place today?

bled honest persons with their false doctrines and outward show of piety. But they have come under God's judgment, and are 'weeping and gnashing their teeth.' Today they bemoan diminishing support by the laity and division in their own ranks. In contrast, Jehovah's wheatlike servants are witnessing joyfully concerning his kingdom. They are shining "as brightly as the sun in the kingdom of their Father."—Matthew 13:40-43; compare Isaiah 65:13, 14.

A SUCCESSFUL 'FISHING' PROJECT

[14] "Again," says Jesus, "the kingdom of the heavens is like a dragnet let down into the sea and gathering up fish of every kind." (Matthew 13:47) Jesus started this 'fishing' project himself, when he called his first disciples from their nets in order to make them "fishers of men." (Matthew 4:19) But during the great apostasy, under angelic surveillance faithful minority groups and Christendom's religions have continued to 'fish' for converts. However, have all of the hundreds of millions of symbolic sea creatures turned out to be 'good fish'? As we have noted, Christendom's religions have based their teachings on the Greek philosophy of Plato, and on the "mysteries" of ancient Babylon. Their fruitage is seen in the hatreds, strife and bloodshed that have spotted the pages of Christendom's history, and in their support of the world wars of our 20th century.

[15] At last, "in the conclusion of the system of

14, 15. (a) How did Jesus start a great 'fishing' project, but what other kinds of 'fishing' have gone on since then, and with what 'catches'? (b) What part do the angels then play, and how do they dispose of the "fish"? (c) For what opportunity should we therefore be thankful?

things," it is time for the angels to haul in the "drag-net." This symbolizes the organizations on earth of those who profess to be followers of Jesus Christ—the true and the false. Those "fish" found to be "unsuitable" for "the kingdom of the heavens" must be thrown away, cast into "the fiery furnace" of destruction. "There is where their weeping and the gnashing of their teeth will be." (Matthew 13:48-50) But the angels are also separating 'good fish' out from the symbolic dragnet. How thankful we should be for our opportunity of being counted along with these—a distinct people dedicated to magnifying Jehovah's name and who pray meaningfully for his kingdom to "come"!

[16] However, what is "the conclusion of the system of things," concerning which Jesus speaks so forcefully in this last parable? What are "the last days," concerning which several of Jesus' disciples wrote? Are we now living in those days? If so, what does this mean for us, and for all mankind?

16. This last parable gives rise to what questions, and why should we be interested in finding the answers?

GIVE HEED TO JESUS' KINGDOM ILLUSTRATIONS!

- These describe the Kingdom as desirable, like a "treasure" or "pearl." Those seeking it are likened to "the right kind of soil," "wheat," "good fish."
- The counterfeit kingdom is portrayed as a mustard "tree" with many branches, a leavened mass of flour. Its supporters are the "birds," "weeds," 'unsuitable fish.'
- Looking at the Kingdom's development from various angles, we are better able to understand the great issue before mankind today, and are encouraged to take a firm and loyal stand for the Kingdom.

CHAPTER 12

THE "LAST DAYS" AND THE KINGDOM

ARE we now living in "the last days"? What do "the last days" mean? Happily, there will be no "last days" for the earth itself. For the Bible assures us: "The earth . . . will not be made to totter to time indefinite, or forever." In line with Jehovah's original purpose, human and animal life will be perpetuated here for all time. (Psalm 104:5-24; 119:89, 90; Genesis 1:27, 28; 8:21, 22) However, there definitely are "last days" for those wicked nations and individuals that are ruining God's earth. It is the 'coming' of the Kingdom that brings ruin to those ruinous ones.—2 Peter 3:3-7; James 5:1-4; Revelation 11:15-18.

[2] Could we now be living in those "last days"? Just take any translation of the Bible and read what the apostle Paul was inspired by God to predict for the "last days," at Second Timothy chapter 3, verses 1 to 5. Then ask yourself, Is this what the world of mankind looks like today? Here, the apostle forecasts "terrible times," and adds:

"People will be lovers of themselves, lovers of money, boastful, proud, abusive, disobedient to their parents, ungrateful,

---

1. (a) What vital questions now arise? (b) What do the Scriptures say about last days [i] for our earth, [ii] for those ruining it?
2. What specifically did Paul foretell for our "terrible times"?

unholy, without love, unforgiving, slanderous, without self-control, brutal, not lovers of the good, treacherous, rash, conceited, lovers of pleasure rather than lovers of God—having a form of godliness but denying its power. Have nothing to do with them."—New International Version.

[3] In writing the above, the apostle was not referring to the "last days" of the Jewish system of things. That could not have been so, for Paul penned those words about the year 65 C.E., when over 30 years of those "last days" had already run their course, and only five years remained until Jerusalem's devastation. Nor had this apostate condition developed yet among professing Christians. Those "last days" of the Jewish system had been bad enough, but they would be far eclipsed by happenings during the "last days" of Satan's entire world system of things, when Jesus would come again to set up his kingdom.

A TWOFOLD FULFILLMENT

[4] In his parables, Jesus had spoken of the "conclusion of the system of things." (Matthew 13:39, 40, 49) Naturally, this aroused his disciples' interest, and especially as the common people were suffering so much, even then, from the harsh rule of Rome and of the Jewish religious leaders. They hoped that God's kingdom would bring relief. Hence, three days before Jesus was put to death, four of his disciples approached him as he was sitting on the Mount of Olives, overlooking Jerusalem, and asked him: "Tell us, When will these things be, and what

---

3. Why must Paul have been referring to "last days" far more momentous than those of the Jewish system?

4. What led up to the disciples' asking the question at Matthew 24:3?

will be the sign of your presence and of the conclusion of the system of things?"—Matthew 24:3; Mark 13:3, 4.

[5] Though Jesus' disciples were thinking only of the immediate future, Jesus' reply on *that* occasion was to have a twofold application: first, during the "last days" of the Jewish system, and, much later, during the "last days" of Satan's world system that embraces the entire inhabited earth.

[6] What Jesus said to those disciples, as recorded at Matthew 24, verses 7 to 22, described the course of events that some of them would observe in a miniature way during the next 37 years down to 70 C.E. For the Jews of Jesus' generation, it was to be a turbulent period of wars, food shortages, earthquakes, hatred of Christians and appearances of false Messiahs. Yet "this good news of the kingdom" would be preached in all creation as a witness. Finally, that "disgusting thing," the pagan Roman army, did indeed invade the "holy place" of Jerusalem's temple. After a brief respite, during which Jesus' disciples were able to obey his prophetic command by fleeing to the mountains for safety, the Romans came again under General Titus. They dashed Jerusalem and its children to the ground and demolished its temple, not leaving a stone upon a stone.—See also Luke 19:43, 44; Colossians 1:23.

[7] In fulfillment of Jesus' "sign," this accumulation of troubles came to afflict the Jews, and was cli-

---

5. How would Jesus' words in reply be fulfilled?
6, 7. (a) How did Jesus' words at Matthew 24:7-22 have a miniature fulfillment? (b) What grim reminder of this remains till now?

maxed by Jerusalem's fiery destruction in 70 C.E. More than a million Jews perished with their city, and the survivors were carried off captive. Titus' victory arch stands in Rome to this day as a grim reminder of the fulfillment of Jesus' prophecy. However, was Jesus' "sign" recorded and preserved in writing as a warning only to persons living in the first century? Is it merely 'dead history' today? The answer must be, No!

A GLOBAL APPLICATION

[8] The miniature fulfillment of Jesus' words during the "last days" of the Jewish system of things should serve to strengthen our belief in the power of divine prophecy. However, those first-century events provide also a striking prophetic pattern of what is to take place on a far wider scale with regard to Satan's global system of things. This must be so, for the execution of God's judgment on Jerusalem in 70 C.E. was not the greatest tribulation up to that time, nor has it been the last. Jesus' words at Matthew 24:21, 22 await their full-scale fulfillment:

"For then there will be great tribulation such as has not occurred since the world's beginning until now, no, nor will occur again. In fact, unless those days were cut short, no flesh would be saved; but on account of the chosen ones those days will be cut short."

[9] The continuing words of Jesus' prophecy, at Matthew 24:23–25:46, indicate also the global scope of "the conclusion of the system of things." When,

8. (a) What effect should the miniature fulfillment of Jesus' words have on us today? (b) What prophetic pattern of greater things does this provide?
9. How do we know that Jesus' words point to a worldwide day of reckoning?

at the climax of that period of distress, the "Son of man," as God's enthroned king, executes judgment on Satan's world, "*all the tribes of the earth* will beat themselves in lamentation." That will embrace all mankind that rejects Jesus' kingship. It is not a judgment involving just one nation and its city, but a worldwide day of reckoning.—Matthew 24:30.

[10] Again indicating the global extent of God's judgment, Jesus' prophecy goes on to compare "the conclusion of the system of things" to the period just preceding the flood of Noah's day, saying:

"For as they were in those days before the flood, eating and drinking, men marrying and women being given in marriage, until the day that Noah entered into the ark; and they took no note until the flood came and swept them all away, so the presence of the Son of man will be."

Even as the Flood of that time wiped out an entire world of godless people, so the fiery tribulation that climaxes Messiah's "presence" will rid our globe of those who ignore the Kingdom in favor of 'doing their own thing.' Happily, many who have 'sought first God's kingdom and his righteousness' will survive to inherit everlasting life in a paradise earth. Will you be one of these?—Matthew 6:33; 24:37-39; 25:31-46.

[11] Numerous prophecies of the Bible show that the coming "great tribulation" will affect "all the nations" on earth. (Psalm 2:2-9; Isaiah 34:1, 2; Jeremiah 25:31-33; Ezekiel 38:23; Joel 3:12-16; Micah

10. (a) As illustrated in Jesus' prophecy, how will the destiny of those who 'do their own thing' differ from that of those 'seeking first God's kingdom'? (b) Why must this be on a global scale?
11. What other prophecies show that all nations are involved, and that there will be survivors?

5:15; Habakkuk 3:1, 12, 13) But there will be survivors!—Isaiah 26:20, 21; Daniel 12:1; Joel 2:31, 32.

THE KING'S PRESENCE IN HEAVENLY GLORY

[12] Jesus' great prophecy on "the sign" of his presence tells us that "when the Son of man arrives in his glory, and all the angels with him, then he will sit down on his glorious throne." (Matthew 25:31) Since the brilliance of that glory would be damaging to mere human eyes, the King must remain invisible to mankind. (Compare Exodus 33:17-20; Hebrews 12:2.) That is why a 'sign of his presence' is needed. At Messiah's second coming it is no longer necessary for him to give up heavenly spirit life in order to appear on earth in a fleshly body, to be used as a "sin offering." Having provided his human sacrifice "once for all time," he comes "the second time . . . apart from sin" as an invisible heavenly king.—Hebrews 7:26, 27; 9:27, 28; 10:8-10; 1 Peter 3:18.

[13] On his last night with his intimate disciples, Jesus had told them: "I am going my way to prepare a place for you. Also, if I go my way and prepare a place for you, I am coming again and will receive you home to myself." (John 14:2, 3) In line with this, Jesus' illustration at Luke 19:11-27 describes him as "a certain man of noble birth [who] traveled to a distant land to secure kingly power for himself and to return." This would take considerable time. But "his citizens hated him and sent out a body of ambassadors after him, to say, 'We do not want this

---

12. (a) Why is a "sign" of Jesus' presence necessary? (b) Why does he not need to appear again in a fleshly body?
13. What does Luke 19:11-27 indicate as to the time of Jesus' return and his acceptance among the nations?

man to become king over us.' " Similarly, there are persons today who claim to be Christian, but who reject "the King of kings" in favor of perpetuating their own imperfect human rulerships. (Revelation 19:16) Like the "citizens" of Jesus' illustration, these will be severely punished.

"A BEGINNING OF PANGS OF DISTRESS"

[14] When does this mighty King, unwanted by the nations, start his reign over our earth? All the evidence points to the year 1914 C.E. But someone will protest, saying, 'Rather than bring in Christ's reign of peace, that year marked the beginning of an era of trouble for mankind!' That is precisely the point! For, according to Bible prophecy, it is when 'the kingdom of the world becomes the kingdom of our Lord Jehovah and of his Christ' that the nations of earth become "wrathful." (Revelation 11:15, 18) It is also the time when Jehovah sends forth his associate king, saying, "Go subduing in the midst of your enemies." (Psalm 110:1, 2) But those enemies are not instantly destroyed.

[15] Revelation chapter 12 describes a breathtaking vision in which the apostle John saw in symbol the birth of God's Messianic kingdom. Like a manchild, this is brought forth from God's "woman" —his heavenly organization of angelic creatures. It is "caught away to God and to his throne," for the Kingdom must be dependent on Jehovah and his sovereignty for its operation.—Revelation 12:1-5.

---

14. Despite protests to the contrary, what favors the year 1914 C.E. as the date for Christ's return?

15. How, appropriately, does Revelation 12 describe the Kingdom's birth?

[16] Next, there is war in heaven! The enthroned King and his angels battle with Satan and his demon hordes, and hurl these out of Jehovah's heavens down to the vicinity of our earth. Hence, it is "woe for the earth and for the sea, because the Devil has come down to you, having great anger, knowing he has a short period of time." (Revelation 12:7-12) During that comparatively "short period," the King gathers righteously inclined humans for salvation and sounds the warning of the impending execution of judgment on Satan's world system of things.—Matthew 24:31-41; 25:31-33.

[17] Today we perceive the fulfillment of Jesus' "sign," as set out in detail at Matthew chapters 24 and 25, Mark chapter 13 and Luke chapter 21. Note that Jesus here describes "a beginning of pangs of distress," in these words:

> ***"Nation will rise against nation, and kingdom against kingdom; and there will be great earthquakes, and in one place after another pestilences and food shortages; and there will be fearful sights and from heaven great signs." (Matthew 24:3, 7, 8; Luke 21:10, 11)***

Did such "pangs of distress" come to plague mankind from 1914 C.E. onward?

[18] It was in the year 1914 that the Great War (later called "World War I") got under way, and with it came pestilence and famine. Writers have found it difficult to describe the utter horror that pervaded the battlefields, as millions perished in trench warfare during the carnage of 1914-1918. In

---

16, 17. (a) What accounts for the woes on earth since 1914? (b) How do Jesus' words in Matthew and Luke describe the start of these distresses?
18. From 1914, how did war become utterly horrible?

the book *Eye Deep in Hell,* Paul Nash is quoted as saying of the European battleground: "No pen or drawing can convey this country—the normal setting of the battles taking place day and night, month after month. Evil and the incarnate fiend alone can be master of this war, and no glimmer of God's hand is seen anywhere. . . . The shells never cease . . . annihilating, maiming, maddening, they plunge into the grave which is this land; one huge grave, and cast upon it the poor dead. It is unspeakable, godless, hopeless."

[19] Also, "earthquakes" are included as part of the "sign." An upsurge in earthquakes since 1914? This may sound surprising. But the statistics are even more surprising! As Geo Malagoli commented in *Il Piccolo:* "During a period of 1,059 years (from 856 to 1914) reliable sources list only 24 major earthquakes." His figures show that during those years an average of 1,800 persons died each year in earthquakes, whereas there have been 43 major earthquakes since 1915, and these have killed an average of 25,300 persons a year.

"FROM HEAVEN GREAT SIGNS"

[20] Jesus prophesied also: "And there will be fearful sights and from heaven great signs." (Luke 21:11) In World War I, the incessant barrages of artillery shells signified something new—*total* warfare. For the first time, the airship and then, more importantly, the airplane opened up the era of aerial

19. What do statistics show as to an upsurge of earthquakes since 1914?

20, 21. (a) What "fearful sights" have become apparent since 1914, and why? (b) What fulfillment of Luke 21:25, 26 do we see today? (c) How have 'great signs from heaven' come increasingly to attention?

warfare. True, in 1914-1918, it was only a beginning, but it would lead to the situation that Jesus describes further on in his prophecy, saying:

"Also, there will be signs in sun and moon and stars, and on the earth anguish of nations, not knowing the way out because of the roaring of the sea and its agitation, while men become faint out of fear and expectation of the things coming upon the inhabited earth; for the powers of the heavens will be shaken."—Luke 21:25, 26.

[21] Man's so-called conquest of space has focused attention on "sun and moon and stars," and there are ominous pointers that the Great Powers intend to use satellites for establishing military springboards. But already they have the know-how for raining down intercontinental ballistic missiles from outer space upon any target of their choice. The present arsenal of nuclear weapons, as stockpiled by opposing nations, is enough to annihilate mankind many times over, and it is estimated that by the turn of the century some 35 nations may be equipped with such weapons of mass destruction.

[22] The "sea," which took on a fresh aspect with the introduction of submarine warfare in World War I, and which brought the United States into the war, is today even more foreboding. Nuclear submarines stand at the ready in the seas. No city on earth is out of range of nuclear missiles. The New York *Times* of August 30, 1980, quoted U.S. State Department expert Marshall D. Shulman as saying that the possibility of a nuclear war "is likely to increase rather than to diminish." A full-page advertisement in the New York *Times* of March 2,

---

22. (a) How has the literal "sea" taken on a new dimension since 1914? (b) What do knowledgeable persons warn concerning the threat to our globe?

WHAT WRITERS HAVE SAID ABOUT 1914

Even after a second world war, many refer back to 1914 as the great turning point in modern history:

"It is indeed the year 1914 rather than that of Hiroshima which marks the turning point in our time."—Rene Albrecht-Carrie, "The Scientific Monthly," July 1951

"Ever since 1914, everybody conscious of trends in the world has been deeply troubled by what has seemed like a fated and pre-determined march toward ever greater disaster. Many serious people have come to feel that nothing can be done to avert the plunge towards ruin. They see the human race, like the hero of a Greek tragedy, driven on by angry gods and no longer the master of fate."—Bertrand Russell, New York "Times Magazine," September 27, 1953

"The modern era . . . began in 1914, and no one knows when or how it will end. . . . It could end in mass annihilation."—Editorial, "The Seattle Times," January 1, 1959

"In 1914 the world, as it was known and accepted then, came to an end."—James Cameron, "1914," published in 1959

"The First World War was one of the great convulsions of history."—Barbara Tuchman, "The Guns of August," 1962

"Thoughts and pictures come to my mind, . . . thoughts from before the year 1914 when there was real peace, quiet and security on this earth—a time when we didn't know fear. . . . Security and quiet have disappeared from the lives of men since 1914."—German statesman Konrad Adenauer, 1965

"The whole world really blew up about World War I and we still don't know why. . . . Utopia was in sight. There was peace and prosperity. Then everything blew up. We've been in a state of suspended animation ever since."—Dr. Walker Percy, "American Medical News," November 21, 1977

"In 1914 the world lost a coherence which it has not managed to recapture since. . . . This has been a time of extraordinary disorder and violence, both across national frontiers and within them."—"The Economist," London, August 4, 1979

"Civilization entered on a cruel and perhaps terminal illness in 1914."—Frank Peters, St. Louis "Post-Dispatch," January 27, 1980

"Everything would get better and better. This was the world I was born in. . . . Suddenly, unexpectedly, one morning in 1914 the whole thing came to an end."—British statesman Harold Macmillan, New York "Times," November 23, 1980

1980, sponsored by more than 600 professional men and women, stated: "Nuclear war, even a 'limited' one, would result in death, injury and disease on a scale that has no precedent in the history of human existence." They added that "an all-out nuclear exchange could be complete in one hour, and could destroy most life in the northern hemisphere." Said the U.S. ambassador to Moscow, in 1981: "I perceive the world to be more dangerous than it has ever been in its history." But expenditure on armaments of mass destruction keeps on spiraling upward.

[23] Mankind appears to be reaching the stage forecast some years ago by Nobel Prize-winner Harold C. Urey, who said: "We will eat fear, sleep fear, live in fear and die in fear." Truly, there is "anguish of nations, not knowing the way out . . . while men become faint out of fear and expectation of the things coming upon the inhabited earth."

[24] Happily, the Sovereign Lord Jehovah, who created this earth for his good purpose, does 'know the way out,' and he will provide that way through the kingdom of his Son. But before we examine in detail the "way out," let us give further attention to Jesus' prophecy, and note how remarkably his words about world war, famine and pestilence, as features of the "sign," parallel a striking prophecy in Revelation. Remember, God's kingdom by Messiah is the remedy—that kingdom for whose 'coming' we earnestly pray!

---

23. In fulfillment of Jesus' prophecy, what stage in history does mankind appear to be reaching?

24. Who knows the "way out," and why should we pray earnestly for the 'coming' of the Kingdom?

CHAPTER 13

THE KINGDOM HORSEMAN RIDES

LET us turn to the fifth chapter of Revelation. Here we read of an inspired vision, given to the apostle John, that is directly related to the 'coming' of God's kingdom. It focuses on the Sovereign Lord Jehovah, "the One seated upon the throne." In his right hand he holds a scroll of writings, "sealed tight with seven seals." But the apostle John gives way to a great deal of weeping. Why? Because, in all the universe, no one could be found that was worthy to unseal the scroll and make known its message. But, look! There *is* someone worthy! He is none other than "the Lion that is of the tribe of Judah," the heir to David's kingdom. —Revelation 5:1-5.

[2] He is worthy because he "has conquered." As a perfect man on earth, he showed unwavering loyalty to his Father, even to a cruel death on a torture stake. "The ruler of the world," Satan, could not break his integrity. Jesus could say: "I have conquered the world."—John 14:30; 16:33.

1, 2. (a) On whom do we now focus attention, and what does he hold in his right hand? (b) Why was John told to stop weeping? (c) Who is the "Lion" of Judah, and why is he worthy to open the seals?

[3] There are others, also, who have conquered the world, and this courageous "Lion," Christ Jesus, counts them as his spiritual "brothers." (Matthew 25:40) By a heavenly resurrection, these are to join him in his 1,000-year Kingdom reign, and share with him in administering the benefits of his ransom sacrifice to the billions of mankind on earth. So voices in heaven are singing a new song. They are saying to this One, who was once led as an innocent lamb to the slaughter:

"You are worthy to take the scroll and open its seals, because you were slaughtered and with your blood you bought persons for God out of every tribe and tongue and people and nation, and you made them to be a kingdom and priests to our God, and they are to rule as kings over the earth." (Revelation 5:9, 10)

What a blessing, that the King and his tried and proved associate kings are about to act on behalf of oppressed humankind! But in this connection, there must first be warfare.

THE RIDER OF THE WHITE HORSE

[4] As the "Lamb" takes the scroll and opens the first seal, a voice thunders from heaven: "Come!" And what do we see? "Look! a white horse"—in symbol of righteous warfare. Its rider has a "bow." He can destroy his enemies from afar—covering much greater distances than mere man-made intercontinental ballistic missiles. A "crown" is given him, and this points to the modern year of 1914,

---

3. Why should we rejoice over the fulfillment of Revelation 5:9, 10?
4. (a) What are symbolized by the "white horse," by the rider's "bow," and by his receiving a "crown"? (b) Who is this rider, and when did he receive kingly authority?

when Jehovah gives him kingly authority over the nations. So much more powerful than puny human lords or kings, this "Lord of lords and King of kings" is to triumph over all enemies of righteousness, along with the "called and chosen and faithful" anointed Christians who are united with him in his heavenly kingdom.—Revelation 6:1, 2; 17:14.

[5] This rider on the "white horse" is a mighty conqueror. What, then, could be more appropriate, as he starts his ride, than that he oust "the original serpent" Satan and his demon angels from heaven? Down to this earth he hurls them! It is no wonder that the Devil now has great anger. As we have already noted, he vents this anger on mankind, making "woe for the earth and for the sea." The Devil knows that he has only "a short period of time," but he is very subtle. He would like to influence *us* into thinking that the "last days" stretch away into the far distant future. Let none of us be lulled to sleep by such thinking!—Revelation 12:9-12; Mark 13:32-37.

A FIERY-COLORED HORSE

[6] The "Lamb" opens the second seal. Out dashes "a fiery-colored horse"! "To the one seated upon it there was granted to take peace away from the earth so that they should slaughter one another; and a great sword was given him." (Revelation 6:4) Ah, the first *world* war of human history bursts upon the scene. Peace is taken away, not merely

---

5. (a) What initial conquest did this rider make? (b) What has been the result to mankind, but why should we heed the warning of Mark 13:32-37?

6. (a) According to Revelation 6:3, 4, what now bursts upon the scene? (b) How was World War I different from all preceding wars?

from a few nations, but from "the earth," as huge armies and navies grapple with one another, using frightful weapons of mass extermination. Whereas previous wars have been fought by professional armies, usually of just a few countries, World War I is *total* warfare. For the first time in history, the entire resources of many nations, including conscripted manpower, are thrown into the battle.

[7] The prophecy mentions "slaughter," and "slaughter" it was! In the battle of the Somme, a new and murderous invention, the machine gun, mowed down British and French troops by the hundreds of thousands, accounting, by some estimates, for 80 percent of all casualties. In nine months at Verdun, more men died than marched with Napoleon's army into Russia. Painted with blood on a cemetery wall, a sign at Verdun read "FIVE KILOMETERS TO THE SLAUGHTERHOUSE." In all, some 9,000,000 soldiers were slaughtered during the four years of that Great War.

[8] Was 1914 the year when the rider of the "fiery-colored horse" took peace away from the earth? Many historians support that view. For example, almost 50 years afterward, the editor of the historical magazine *American Heritage* wrote: "In the summer of 1914 the nations were at peace and the future seemed serene. Then the guns spoke, and things would never again be the same. . . . The year 1914 was one of the most fateful years in human history . . . In that year there came one of those profound turning points that occur no more than once or twice in a millennium. Probably it

---

7-9. With regard to "slaughter," what statistics and statements show that 1914 marked the beginning of the most murderous period of all history?

will be a long time before we fully understand what 1914 got us into, but we can at least begin to see what it wrenched us out of." Truly, the rider of the "fiery-colored horse" wrenched peace from the earth, and 1914 was the year.

9 The horseman has continued his murderous ride through a second world war, in which 16,000,000 soldiers died in battle. As we move on in the 1980's, a Hungarian professor calculates that in three decades following the end of World War II, another 25,000,000 soldiers died in battle. He states that during the 33 years that followed the close of World War II, there were only 26 days in which there was no war somewhere in the world.

10 The prophecy tells us that "a *great* sword" was given to this horseman. And, indeed, lethal weaponry has played a big part in the slaughter of the wars of this 20th century. In World War I, poison gas, automatic weapons, army tanks, airplanes and submarines made their first full-scale debut. In World War II, aerial warfare literally wiped out cities, most of the casualties being innocent women, children and old folk. In one night the city of Coventry, England, was devastated, and later an air attack by the Allies snuffed out 135,000 lives in Dresden, Germany. There followed the mass extermination by atomic bombs of at least 92,000 persons in Hiroshima and 40,000 in Nagasaki, Japan, again mostly civilians. What the "great sword" might accomplish today if nuclear warfare erupted beggars the imagination!

---

10. How has this horseman used "a great sword"?

"LOOK! A BLACK HORSE"

[11] As the "Lamb" opens the third seal, "a black horse" charges forth. "And the one seated upon it had a pair of scales in his hand." (Revelation 6:5) Ah, here is a companion rider to the horseman of total warfare! This is the horseman that brings famine. During both the world wars, famine conditions plagued many countries. Food rationing, as represented by the "pair of scales," became the norm for the citizens of the warring nations. And in the wake of World War I came the greatest famine of all history. *The Nation* of June 7, 1919, reported that 32,000,000 people in India were "on the verge of starvation." *World's Work* of March 1921 stated that in northern China alone 15,000 people were dying every day from hunger. The New York *Times* publication *Current History Magazine* of October 1921 quoted a British report that in Russia "no fewer than 35,000,000 people are stalked by the grim spectre of famine and pestilence." Similar famine conditions prevailed following World War II, when *Look* magazine of June 11, 1946, reported: "A fourth of the world is starving today."

[12] Even without total war, a crop failure in our modern world often brings news headlines such as this one in 1974: "India under the third horseman's shadow." In 1976: "An Ever-Hungrier World Faces Major Food Crisis." And in 1979: "450 million people are starving." As the world population multiplies, the food situation in underdeveloped and war-torn countries becomes ever more desperate. The Atlas World Press Review, in the *New Scien-*

11, 12. (a) How has the rider of the "black horse" shown himself to be a companion to the second horseman? (b) What shows that his ride has continued until our day?

tist of May 1975, stated: "The world faces a double-headed specter. Famine is only one of its aspects: the other is chronic malnutrition. FAO [Food and Agriculture Organization] estimates that 61 out of 97 developing nations produced or imported substantially less food in 1970 than was necessary to feed their populations. On a conservative estimate, FAO reckons 460 million people suffer from malnutrition; a more liberal interpretation might put the figure at 1 billion." Now, in the 1980's, the situation is far worse.

[13] As the third horseman continues his ride, a voice from the heavens cries: "A quart of wheat for a denarius, and three quarts of barley for a denarius; and do not harm the olive oil and the wine." (Revelation 6:6) With a denarius representing a day's wage, a workman would indeed be incensed at this highly inflated price. And does not inflation continue to make inroads into the income of ordinary people today? But what of those items such as the "oil" and the "wine"? Greedy profiteers and other wealthy persons would like to protect their affluent way of life. But will they succeed? We shall see, as the "black horse" charges to and fro throughout the earth.

13. What modern-day conditions and fears are foreshadowed at Revelation 6:6?

THE BLACK HORSE CONTINUES ITS GALLOP

"The World Bank estimates 780 million people around the world are living in absolute poverty, a condition that is 'beneath any reasonable definition of human decency.' "—Detroit "Free Press," September 1, 1980

'A PALE HORSE, WITH DEATH'

[14] The fourth seal is opened, and "a pale horse" joins the galloping steeds. The rider is Death. Closely following comes Hades—whether on another horse or not, the record does not say. But they have a gruesome commission: "Authority was given them over the fourth part of the earth, to kill with a long sword and with food shortage and with deadly plague and by the wild beasts of the earth." (Revelation 6:7, 8) Since that fateful year 1914, the presence of Death and Hades has indeed spread to the four corners of the earth.

[15] "Deadly plague"! They called it the 1918-1919 pandemic, or the Spanish flu. In a few weeks, its victims were double the number that had died on the battlefields of World War I—a staggering total of at least 21,000,000. In the United States the official figure for flu deaths was 548,452, more than 10 times the number of American soldiers killed in the war. For the most part its victims were the young and virile. In India, more than 12,000,000 died. It spared no continent or island—with the one exception of the island of St. Helena. Entire villages among the Eskimos and in Central Africa were wiped out. In Tahiti, funeral pyres were used to dispose of the bodies of 4,500 persons who died in just 15 days, and in Western Samoa 7,500 out of a population of 38,000 perished from the plague.

[16] However, the Spanish flu has not been the only death-dealing disease brought forth by the rider of

---

14. How do the rider of the fourth horse and his companion aptly tie in with events since 1914?

15, 16. (a) What striking fulfillment did this prophecy have in 1918-1919? (b) What shows that this horse has been galloping continuously since 1914?

the "pale horse." The New York *Times* reported that in 1915, in the battle for Gallipoli, dysentery killed more soldiers than did bullets. From 1914 to 1923 cholera killed 3,250,000 in India. In 1915 "from two and one-half to three million deaths" in Russia were attributed to typhus. And as the rider gallops on into more recent times, heart disease and cancer have become leading killers, syphilis "the No. 2 Killer Among Communicable Diseases" and hepatitis "a Worldwide Explosion of Disease."

RELIEF AT HAND!

[17] Now for more than 60 years, the "fiery-colored horse," the "black horse" and the "pale horse" have been riding neck and neck, with Hades closely following. Indeed, Hades has reaped a bumper crop of casualties, running into the hundreds of millions. It is of interest that a former president of the United States, Herbert Hoover, linked together these three horsemen, saying in 1941: "The consequences of great wars are always famine and pestilence . . . The World War of twenty-five years ago brought hunger to 300,000,000 people. . . . After a year and a half of the present war [World War II] nearly 100,000,000 more people are short of food than after three years of the last war." What disaster a third world war would mean for mankind!

[18] The world's leaders are fully aware of the havoc created by the riders of the "fiery-colored," the "black" and the "pale" horses. However, they ignore the Rider of the "white horse." The joyful day approaches for this glorious King to take action

17, 18. (a) What did one statesman say, indicating the link between the second, third and fourth horsemen? (b) But whom do the world's leaders ignore? (c) Why can we be joyful about what the glorious King will do?

in reversing the order of things! Instead of war, he will bring in peace. In place of famine, he will provide plenty. In lieu of disease, he will restore mankind to perfect health, and even Hades will deliver up the dead. A parallel passage in the Psalms describes this rider on the "white horse" in these words:

> ***"Gird your sword upon your thigh, O mighty one, with your dignity and your splendor. And in your splendor go on to success; ride in the cause of truth and humility and righteousness, and your right hand will instruct you in fear-inspiring things." (Psalm 45:3, 4)***

The Kingdom Horseman's triumph draws near!

[19] Let us not be unduly perturbed, therefore, by the worsening situation on earth today. Rather, may our viewpoint be similar to that of one of Jehovah's Witnesses who, because of her beliefs, spent 20 of the years 1956 to 1978 in prison in a socialistic country. At one stage she was under sentence of death, and to this day she carries torture marks on her arms. How did she keep strong in faith? It was by meditating on the many Scripture passages that she remembered from her previous diligent study of the Bible. She says that one of these was Revelation 6:2. She was firmly convinced that the Rider of the "white horse," the King Jesus Christ, had been enthroned in the heavens in 1914, and she was determined to endure until he should "complete his conquest." May all others who pray for God's kingdom to "come" remain faithful until the King is completely victorious!

---

19. (a) In view of the fulfillment of Revelation 6:2-8, should we be perturbed? (b) What example is cited to encourage us to be strong in faith?

CHAPTER 14

THE KING REIGNS!

UNQUESTIONABLY, the year 1914 marked a major turning point in the affairs of the nations and of mankind. But it was far more significant than most historians realize. It was a time when thrilling events took place related to the 'coming' of God's kingdom. Years in advance, careful Bible students were looking forward with keen anticipation to that year. On what basis?

[2] Thirty-four years before 1914, the magazine *Zion's Watch Tower and Herald of Christ's Presence*, in its issues of December 1879 and March 1880, was pointing to 1914 as a marked date in Bible prophecy. An article in its issue of June 1880 called attention to the approaching end of "the Times of the Gentiles (Luke xxi. 24)." Though the writer at the time did not understand the full implication of events about to take place, he showed from Bible chronology that a period of "seven times," or 2,520 years, of domination in government by godless nations, starting from the first desolating of ancient Jerusalem, was due to end in "A. D. 1914." He stated: "The long period of 2520 years and . . . bitter experience [of God's people] under the dominion of the beasts, (human govern-

---

1, 2. (a) What greater significance was there to the year 1914? (b) How did the *Watch Tower* magazine pinpoint 1914 many years in advance?

ments, Dan. vii.) is clearly represented in Dan. iv., by the 'seven times' of Nebuchadnezzar and his bitter experience among the beasts." What, then, are the "seven times"?

INTERPRETING A DREAM

[3] Chapter 4 of the Bible book of Daniel describes a remarkable prophetic dream. It illustrates that "the Most High is Ruler in the kingdom of mankind, and that to the one whom he wants to he gives it." (Daniel 4:25) Nebuchadnezzar, king of Babylon, had the dream and related it to the prophet Daniel for interpretation.

[4] Nebuchadnezzar saw in vision an immense tree that was visible to the extremity of the earth. It provided food for all, and shelter. But a "holy one" from heaven decreed that the tree be chopped down and its stump banded with iron and copper, the two strongest metals of the time. "Seven times" were to pass by while the tree was in this restrained state.

[5] Interpreting this prophetic vision, Daniel explained that the tree in its grandeur pictured Nebuchadnezzar. He was to be 'chopped down' or brought low. "Seven times" would pass by during which Nebuchadnezzar would be like the beasts of the field. But just as the "tree" was not destroyed completely, so after the "seven times" the king would be restored.—Daniel 4:19-27.

[6] This is precisely what befell Nebuchadnezzar.

---

3. What fundamental truth is stated at Daniel 4:25?
4-6. (a) What dream did Nebuchadnezzar have? (b) How did Daniel interpret it? (c) How was it fulfilled? (d) On being restored, what recognition did Nebuchadnezzar make?

He was debased, and became like an animal removed from human habitation, eating vegetation. Those "seven times" were evidently seven years, during which Nebuchadnezzar had 'his bitter experience among the beasts.' His own hair grew long, just like eagles' feathers, and his nails grew to be like birds' claws. But finally he regained his sanity and was restored to his kingship. When that occurred, he praised and glorified "the King of the heavens" as the One who really exercises rulership and whose "kingdom is for generation after generation."—Daniel 4:28-37.

[7] However, what has all of this to do with the year 1914 of our Common Era?

"THE APPOINTED TIMES OF THE NATIONS"

[8] It was while describing 'the sign of the conclusion of the system of things' that Jesus Christ said:

"Jerusalem will be trampled on by the nations, until the appointed times of the nations are fulfilled." (Luke 21:24)

The "nations" referred to by Jesus were the non-Jewish nations, or "Gentiles." The well-known King James Version of the Bible here uses the expression "times of the Gentiles." Thus, many have wondered, 'What are the Gentile Times? What time period did Jesus have in mind? When did it begin, and when would it end?'

[9] We have already seen that Jesus' great prophecy on the "sign" has vital meaning for us today. So we need to know, also, the answers to these questions.

7-9. (a) In which prophecy did Jesus refer to the end of the Gentile Times? (b) So what questions should be of vital interest to us?

"JERUSALEM" MEANS WHAT?

[10] In commenting on Jesus' prophecy, Professor A. T. Robertson* observes that Jesus used "the destruction of the temple and of Jerusalem which did happen in that generation in A.D. 70, as also a symbol of his second coming and of the end of the world or consummation of the age." Therefore, we may ask: Aside from what befell Jerusalem in 70 C.E., what larger or long-range meaning could Jesus have been attaching to "Jerusalem" at Luke 21:24?

[11] Jesus regarded Jerusalem as Israel's capital city, where kings anointed by Jehovah in the line of David sat "upon Jehovah's throne," ruling as kings for Jehovah God. Also, its temple was the center of true worship for all the earth. (1 Chronicles 28:5; 29:23; 2 Chronicles 9:8) The *Cyclopaedia* by M'Clintock and Strong observes: "Jerusalem had been made the imperial residence of the king of all Israel; and the Temple, often called 'the house of Jehovah,' constituted at the same time the residence of the King of kings, the supreme head of the theocratical state, . . . Jerusalem was not, indeed, politically important: it was not the capital of a powerful empire directing the affairs of other states, but it stood high in the bright prospects foretold by David when declaring his faith in the coming of a Messiah [Psalm 2:6; 110:2]."—Volume IV, page 838.

---

* *Word Pictures in the New Testament*, Vol. I, p. 188.

10-12. (a) According to one scholar, of what were the events of 29-70 C.E. a type? (b) But what larger meaning could "Jerusalem" take on at Luke 21:24? (c) How does a well-known cyclopedia help us with this viewpoint? (d) For what does "Jerusalem" thus stand?

[12] The fact that the kings in David's line sat on "the throne of the kingship of Jehovah" underscored the truth that the kingdom really was God's. The kingdom of Israel as centered in Jerusalem was a typical kingdom of God. "Jerusalem" thus stood for the kingdom of God.

[13] Recall, now, Jesus' words: "Jerusalem will be trampled on by the nations, until the appointed times of the nations are fulfilled." (Luke 21:24) When did this 'trampling' begin? Clearly, it began long before Jesus was born in Bethlehem, for human kings in the line of David had long since ceased to reign in Jerusalem. The Davidic dynasty of kings came to an end when King Zedekiah was dethroned by the invading Babylonians under Nebuchadnezzar.

[14] The Bible's accurate history tells us what happened because of the badness of the people and of King Zedekiah. It states: "The rage of Jehovah came up against his people, until there was no healing. So he brought up against them the king of the Chaldeans [Babylonians], who proceeded to kill their young men with the sword . . . Everything [God] gave into [Nebuchadnezzar's] hand. And all the utensils, great and small, of the house of the true God and the treasures of the house of Jehovah and the treasures of the king and of his princes, everything he brought to Babylon. And he proceeded to burn the house of the true God and pull down the wall of Jerusalem." (2 Chronicles 36:11, 12, 16-20) There the 'trampling' began.

13, 14. When and how did the 'trampling' of Luke 21:24 begin?

"TRAMPLED" FOR HOW LONG?

[15] The prophet Ezekiel foretold the dethroning of Zedekiah, the last of the Davidic line of kings to rule from earthly Jerusalem, in these words:

> ***"This is what the Sovereign Lord Jehovah has said, 'Remove the turban, and lift off the crown. This will not be the same. . . . A ruin, a ruin, a ruin I shall make it. As for this also, it will certainly become no one's until he comes who has the legal right, and I must give it to him.'"—Ezekiel 21:26, 27.***

[16] Though King Zedekiah then lost the "legal right" to the Davidic kingdom, the promised Messiah would regain that "right" and rule in the kingdom of God "forever." (Luke 1:32, 33) But how long would it be until the Messianic kingdom—which had been typified by the earthly kingdom of Israel with its capital at Jerusalem—began to rule?

[17] Jehovah God knew, and he could indicate the time period in his Word, just as he had foretold many other future things. In his discourse on "the conclusion of the system of things," Jesus several times referred to Daniel's prophecy, in which God had accurately foretold many coming developments in heaven and on earth. (Compare Matthew 24:3, 15, 21, 30 with Daniel 9:27; 11:31; 12:1; 7:13.) Also, had not the prophecy of the "seventy weeks," at Daniel 9:24-27, provided the accurate timetable for Messiah's first coming? Would it not be appropriate for the same prophet to give the timing for the second coming of Messiah? It is in Daniel the fourth chapter that we find this prophetic information that concerns us directly.

15-17. (a) Who lost the "legal right" to David's kingdom, and how? (b) Who would regain that right, and for how long? (c) So what pertinent question arises? (d) Why would it be appropriate for Daniel to answer this question?

MAJOR FULFILLMENT

[18] We have already examined the initial, typical application of Daniel's prophecy of the "seven times" and have noted that it applied to the seven literal years of Nebuchadnezzar's madness. The fact that secular history gives no detailed account of Nebuchadnezzar's seven-year absence from the throne should not be surprising. Ancient records of Egypt, Assyria and Babylon are notorious for their omission of anything that might be embarrassing to the ruler, which is one reason for their not being as reliable as God's inspired Word. It is God's Word that assures us that the dream vision was fulfilled. The language of the prophecy also indicates that there would be an even more far-reaching fulfillment, and that has likewise taken place. In what way?

[19] It should be noted that the dream was given to the king of Babylon, the very world ruler that was instrumental in overthrowing the typical kingdom of God on earth, thus establishing world dominion by Gentile rule. Also, the vision was given evidently not many years after this monumental change took place—when there had ceased to be a typical kingdom through which Jehovah exercised sovereignty. Further, Daniel chapter 4 repeatedly emphasizes the theme 'that the Most High is the Ruler in the kingdom of mankind and gives it to whom he wants.' (Daniel 4:17, 26, 34, 35) Thus we have good

---

18. (a) Why may it be that secular histories fail to mention Nebuchadnezzar's madness? (b) Why should we heed what God's Word here says?

19. Why, logically, would this vision help us to determine the length of the Gentile Times?

reason to look to this vision for information on the duration of Gentile domination of the earth.

[20] Counting from the time that God's typical kingdom, with its Davidic king, was overthrown, how long would it be until God once again expressed his sovereignty through a kingdom involving the royal line of David, with Messiah as the ruling king? Daniel chapter 4 provides a basis for determining the length of the Gentile Times or "the appointed times of the nations," during which those nations would trample on "Jerusalem," or the kingdom of God.—Luke 21:24.

[21] This trampling dates from the year in which Nebuchadnezzar removed King Zedekiah from the throne in Jerusalem. From then on, Jehovah's exercise of sovereignty as represented in the line of Judean kings was 'chopped down.' It was under restraint, like the banded tree trunk of Nebuchadnezzar's dream. Beastlike Gentile powers held sway over all the earth. But there existed a hope for the "tree," that it would "sprout again." And then people living would "know that the Most High is Ruler in the kingdom of mankind."—Daniel 4:15-17; Job 14:7; compare Isaiah 11:1, 2; 53:2.

[22] In this restored kingdom, the Most High rules by his Messiah. No, not at that One's first appearance as a perfect man on earth, when the Jews despised him and rejected him as king. But the bands on the

---

20. What question do we ask, and where may we look for the answer?
21. What do Daniel 4:15-17 and Job 14:7 indicate as to the situation following Zedekiah's dethronement?
22. When and in what way does the Kingdom "tree" flourish again?

tree stump are released, and the Kingdom "tree" flourishes again, when this "lowliest one of mankind" arrives in his glory as heavenly King of the people of all nations. Then, as the Gentile Times end, the kingdom of the world becomes "the kingdom of our Lord and of his Christ."—Revelation 11:15; Daniel 4:17, 25.

THE "SEVEN TIMES"—HOW LONG?

[23] Obviously, then, the "seven times" as applied to the Gentile Times must be much longer than seven literal years. Remember, Jesus spoke of the 'fulfilling' or ending of these Gentile Times in connection with "the conclusion of the system of things." (Luke 21:7, 24; Matthew 24:3) So they must reach down to our day. Just how long are they?

[24] Turning to chapter 12 of Revelation, we note that verses 6 and 14 show a period of 1,260 days to be "a time and times and half a time," or 1 + 2 + ½ for a total of 3½ times. Therefore, "a time" would be equal to 360 days, or 12 lunar months averaging 30 days each. "Seven times" would come to 2,520 days; and the Biblical prophetic reckoning

23. Why must the Gentile Times reach down to our day?
24. How may we interpret the length of the "seven times"?

CALCULATING THE "SEVEN TIMES"

7 "times" = 7 × 360 = 2,520 years

(a Biblical "time" or year being the mean between a lunar year of 354 days and a solar year of 365¼ days)

607 B.C.E. to 1 B.C.E. =	606 years
1 B.C.E. to 1 C.E. =	1 year
1 C.E. to 1914 C.E. =	1,913 years
607 B.C.E. to 1914 C.E. =	2,520 years

of "a day for a year, a day for a year," indicates that these actually would work out to be a period of 2,520 calendar years. (Numbers 14:34; Ezekiel 4:6) This, therefore, is the duration of the "seven times"—the Gentile Times.

[25] We are helped to fix the calendar date for the start of the Gentile Times by consulting God's Word. As we have already noted, Jehovah allowed the Babylonians to conquer his people, destroy Jerusalem and its temple, remove Zedekiah from "the throne of the kingship of Jehovah" and take the Jews into Babylonian exile. (1 Chronicles 28:5) Events that followed "in the seventh month" led the few Jews who had remained in the land to flee to Egypt, so that Judah then lay completely desolate. (2 Kings 25:1-26; Jeremiah 39:1-10; 41:1–43:7) Jehovah's prophet Jeremiah had foretold that the desolation would last for 70 years. (Jeremiah 25:8-11) Then Jehovah would 'call to account against the king of Babylon his error' and 'bring His people back to this place,' their homeland.—Jeremiah 25:12; 29:10.

[26] Daniel himself lived in Babylonian exile for many years. On the night that Babylon fell to the Medo-Persians, he was an eyewitness to the fulfillment of his own prophecy, and of other prophecies, against that city. (Daniel 5:17, 25-30; Isaiah 45:1, 2) Historians calculate that Babylon fell in early October of the year 539 B.C.E. Soon thereafter, Daniel discerned from Jeremiah's prophecy that the 70-year

---

25. How do the "seventy years" of Jeremiah 25:11 figure in determining the start of the Gentile Times?

26. (a) Of what was Daniel an eyewitness, and what did he discern? (b) How may we know the month and the year that Daniel's restoration prophecy was fulfilled? (c) Specifically, what is that date?

captivity and desolation for Jerusalem was about ended. (Daniel 9:2) And he was right! In the first year of Cyrus the Persian, which most historians date from the spring of 538 B.C.E., Cyrus issued a decree permitting the Jews to return to their homeland to repopulate it and to rebuild Jehovah's temple there. (2 Chronicles 36:20-23; Ezra 1:1-5) The inspired historical account tells us that the Jews responded readily to Cyrus' decree, so that "when the seventh month arrived the sons of Israel were in their cities." (Ezra 3:1) By our calendar that would be October, 537 B.C.E., which date therefore marks the completion of the foretold 70 years of desolation.

[27] That historical information is important to us in determining the beginning of "the appointed times of the nations." Since the 70 years of desolation for Judah and Jerusalem ended in 537 B.C.E., they began in 607 B.C.E. That would be the year when Zedekiah ceased to sit upon the "throne of the kingship of Jehovah" in Jerusalem. It therefore marks also the date for the beginning of the Gentile Times. Counting from October 607 B.C.E., the "seven times" of 2,520 years bring us down to early October 1914 C.E., when, as we have already seen, Jesus' great prophecy on "the conclusion of the system of things" started to be fulfilled. Reliable information in God's Word is the basis for this conclusion, which the *Watchtower* magazine has been championing now for more than 100 years.

---

27. (a) When, then, must the 70 years have had their start, and with what event? (b) How long were the "seven times," and when therefore must they have ended? (c) What other great prophecy started to undergo fulfillment at that exact date? (d) What information has *The Watchtower* been championing for 100 years and more?

[28] Thankful, indeed, we can be that Jehovah preserved in his inspired Word an accurate picture of the needed details involving the Jews, the Babylonians and the Medo-Persians in the sixth century B.C.E. Otherwise it would be difficult to piece together the exact timing of events back there, for secular records of that period are certainly incomplete.

[29] However, based primarily on such secular records, some persons figure that Jerusalem was destroyed in 587/6 B.C.E. and that the Jews came under Babylonian domination in Nebuchadnezzar's accession year, which they calculate as being 605 B.C.E.* They thus hold 605 B.C.E. to be the date when Jeremiah 25:11 began to be fulfilled: "All the land shall be a desolation; and they shall serve among the Gentiles seventy years." (Bagster's *Greek Septuagint*) If that were so and the Gentile Times were counted from then, it would put the end of the prophetic "seven times" in the World War year of 1916. Yet, as stated, we believe that there is much stronger reason for accepting the information in God's inspired Word, which points to the Gentile Times' beginning in October 607 B.C.E. and ending in October of 1914 C.E.

[30] We can be happy that God long ago had recorded in his Word prophecies that so clearly give the timing of Jesus' coming as Messiah in 29 C.E., and

* See Appendix, page 186.

28, 29. (a) What is it about secular records that should make us thankful for the details preserved in God's Word? (b) Why is there strong reason for preferring October 1914 over other dates for the end of the Gentile Times?
30. What combined events identify the period from 1914 as the "last days"?

also of his "presence" as glorious heavenly King from 1914 C.E. While "the conclusion of the system of things" runs its course, we see intensifying all around us the conditions for which Jesus told us to watch. The world wars, the famines, the pestilences, the earthquakes, the lawlessness, the lovelessness, the hatreds and persecution of those who stand for Bible principles—all of these in combination have identified for us the "last days."—2 Timothy 3:1; Matthew 24:3-12; Mark 13:7-13.

THE MILLENNIUM—WHEN?

[31] How long will this fearful situation last? With Christ Jesus now enthroned as Warrior-King, there is good reason to believe that it will not be long before he executes judgment on God's enemies. "Concerning that day or the hour nobody knows," so that we gain nothing by speculating. Nevertheless, we should heed Jesus' counsel: "Keep on the watch." (Mark 13:32; Matthew 24:42) As we view the worsening conditions on earth and experience how people in general are unresponsive to the Kingdom good news, we may be inclined to ask, as did God's prophet, concerning our preaching: "How long, O Jehovah?" To which Jehovah replies:

"Until the cities actually crash in ruins, to be without an inhabitant, and the houses be without earthling man, and the ground itself is ruined into a desolation." (Isaiah 6:10-12)

At his appointed time Jehovah will carry out this execution of judgment, first upon Christendom and then on all other segments of Satan's world. Christ's

31. (a) What counsel does Jesus give for our day, and why? (b) What question may we be inclined to ask, and what is Jehovah's reply?

1,000-year reign of peace will follow immediately. —Revelation 20:1-3, 6.

"THIS GENERATION"—WHICH?

32 In his great prophecy on the "sign," Jesus assures us: "Truly I say to you that this generation will by no means pass away until all these things occur." (Matthew 24:34) Since he does not apply any specific length of time to a generation, what are we to understand by "this generation"?

33 In Jesus' day, some of the disciples who heard his words, and others of his contemporaries, survived to live through the final "tribulation" on the Jewish system of things. They were the "generation" of Jesus' time. At this writing, in the United States alone there are more than 10,000,000 persons still living who were old enough to observe "a beginning of pangs of distress" in 1914-1918. Some of these may still survive quite a number of years. Yet

> **"THE GENERATION OF 1914"**
>
> In a book of the above title, Robert Wohl "suggests that generations are not mathematically definable in terms of numbers of years, but cluster around major historical crises, of which the first world war is the supreme example."—"The Economist," March 15, 1980

Jesus assures us that, before "this generation" passes away, he will come as "Son of man" to execute judgment on Satan's system of things. (Matthew 24:8, 21, 37-39) We should keep awake, expectant of that 'coming of the kingdom.'—Luke 21:31-36.

---

32. What question arises in view of Matthew 24:34?
33. (a) What was the "generation" of Jesus' time? (b) Correspondingly, what may be said of the "generation" of 1914-1918?

CHAPTER 15

LOYAL ADVOCATES OF THE KINGDOM

LONG in advance, Daniel's prophecy had pinpointed 29 C.E. as the year of Messiah's appearing as a man, and also 1914 C.E. as the year of his enthronement in heavenly glory. Further, Daniel foretold in detail how the great controversy over world domination will be settled.

[2] Now the great issue of rightful rulership of earth must be judged to a finality. But in which court? Why, in the highest court of all the universe! Daniel describes it in these words:

"I kept on beholding until there were thrones placed and the Ancient of Days sat down. His clothing was white just like snow, and the hair of his head was like clean wool. His throne was flames of fire; its wheels were a burning fire. There was a stream of fire flowing and going out from before him. There were a thousand thousands that kept ministering to him, and ten thousand times ten thousand that kept standing right before him. The Court took its seat, and there were books that were opened."—Daniel 7:9, 10.

[3] The "King of eternity," Jehovah God, proceeds thus to sit in judgment. (Revelation 15:3) But what

1. What major events did Daniel foretell?
2. What issue must now be judged, and in which court?
3. (a) Who is the Judge? (b) What do the "books" show? (c) What judgment is passed?

are the "books" that now lie open before him? They are the miserable record of rulership that the nations have made down through history. With the Gentile Times ending in 1914 C.E., "the Court" properly takes away the authority of "their rulerships," though there is "a lengthening in life given to them for a time and a season"—until judgment is actually executed on them at Armageddon.—Daniel 7:12; Revelation 16:14, 16.

[4] To whom, then, shall rulership be given? Daniel continues:

> ***"I kept on beholding in the visions of the night, and, see there! with the clouds of the heavens someone like a son of man happened to be coming; and to the Ancient of Days he gained access, and they brought him up close even before that One. And to him there were given rulership and dignity and kingdom, that the peoples, national groups and languages should all serve even him. His rulership is an indefinitely lasting rulership that will not pass away, and his kingdom one that will not be brought to ruin."—Daniel 7:13, 14.***

[5] Who is this "someone like a son of man"? It is none other than the glorified Lord Jesus Christ. Since "the clouds of the heavens" symbolize invisibility, it is with the discerning eye of faith that we perceive the heavenly "sign" of his presence, along with the "sign" that became apparent in events on earth at the "beginning of pangs of distress" in 1914 C.E.—Matthew 24:3, 7, 8, 30; Revelation 1:7.

[6] We note from Daniel's prophecy that judgment is next given "in favor of the holy ones of the Supreme One," and that these, too, receive "the

---

4, 5. (a) To whom is rulership given? (b) How only may we discern the King's presence?
6. (a) With regard to whom else is judgment passed? (b) What do these receive, and how?

kingdom and the rulership and the grandeur of the kingdoms under all the heavens." (Daniel 7:22, 27) Who are these "holy ones"? Obviously, they contrast with the corrupt, self-seeking rulers in human government, who have for so long oppressed the people. They are none other than the 144,000 anointed "holy ones," humans that are "without blemish" as to their integrity and that are "bought from among mankind" to become corulers with "the Son of man" in his heavenly kingdom. They are resurrected to be with him "at the last day." (Revelation 14:3-5; Matthew 24:30; John 6:40) At Jesus' coming into his kingdom, a remnant of these "holy ones" are found to be very much alive on earth. And they have a work to do!

CHAMPIONING GOD'S WORD

[7] As the time approached for "the Son of man" to receive his kingdom, it was apparently God's will that a preparatory work be done here on earth. In the 1870's Charles T. Russell organized a small group of dedicated Christians in Pittsburgh, Pennsylvania, U.S.A. These soon came to realize that Christendom's religions were based on Babylonian doctrine and ritual, along with Plato's teaching of the immortal soul, and not on God's Word. Casting aside false religion, this small group became staunch advocates of the Bible's teachings of Jesus' ransom, the resurrection and God's kingdom as the hope for suffering mankind.

[8] Through the *Watchtower* magazine, which has been published continuously since July 1879, Rus-

---

7, 8. (a) What group started a preparatory work, and when? (b) What did they cast aside? (c) What did they staunchly advocate? (d) To what date did they point forward? (e) What instrument have they used in advertising God's kingdom?

sell and his companions forthrightly championed the Bible teaching of creation as against Darwin's theory of evolution. They 'turned the hose on hell' by showing from the Bible that there never has been a fiery place of torment for 'departed souls,' but that the Bible "hell" is the grave. (Psalm 16:10; Acts 2:29-32) They pointed forward to 1914 C.E. as a marked date in connection with the 'coming' of God's kingdom. To this day, *The Watchtower Announcing Jehovah's Kingdom*, published in more than 100 different languages, and in the millions of copies each issue, loyally advocates God's kingdom by Christ as the only hope of the nations of mankind.—Matthew 12:21; Psalm 145:10-12.

⁹ After serving faithfully for more than 30 years as the first president of the Watch Tower Society, C. T. Russell died on October 31, 1916, and was succeeded by J. F. Rutherford. Religious clergymen were using the war situation to whip up opposition to the Kingdom message. Christian meetings were broken up. In a number of countries, faithful servants of God were imprisoned. Rutherford and seven other responsible ministers from the Watch Tower headquarters at Brooklyn, New York, U.S.A., were sentenced to many years in jail. However, these servants of God were not dismayed, for Bible prophecy had foretold such persecutions. For example, Revelation 11:7-12 describes the worldly nations, under the symbol of a "beast," as making war against God's "witnesses," to "conquer them and kill them." Their prophesying would be stopped, and figuratively they would be like corpses exposed long enough to become a stench in the "broad way" of Christendom. All of this happened,

---

9. How was Revelation 11:7-12 fulfilled toward these "witnesses"?

as God's servants worldwide were held up to public ridicule. However, as war hysteria died down, and as those imprisoned were released—completely exonerated of the false charges against them—"spirit of life from God entered into them." They were elevated to a position of divine favor, and from 1919 they entered on a period of zealous Kingdom activity.—Isaiah 52:7, 8; Romans 10:15.

"BABYLON THE GREAT" FALLS!

[10] During those war years, not only did the clergy of Christendom take the lead in persecuting true Christians, but they also rejected the evidence that God's kingdom was at hand. They had their own religious "kingdom," that of "Babylon the Great." (Revelation 17:5, 6, 18) On both sides of the war, they preached the youth into the trenches and gave wholehearted support to that terrible slaughter. For such action, Christendom's clergy must still carry a heavy bloodguilt, like those religious leaders of ancient Jerusalem, to whom Jehovah's prophet said: "In your skirts there have been found the blood marks of the souls of the innocent poor ones." —Jeremiah 2:34; 19:3, 4; see also Matthew 23:34, 35.

[11] This bloodguilt was now added to Christendom's idolatry and her teaching of false Babylonish doctrines. Hence, the prophet Ezekiel's words came also to apply to apostate Christendom:

"This is what the Sovereign Lord Jehovah has said: 'O city that is shedding blood in her midst till her time comes, and that has made dungy idols within herself in order to become unclean, by your blood that you have shed you have become guilty, and by your dungy idols that you have made you have

---

10. What guilt did Christendom's religions incur, and how?
11. How does Ezekiel 22:3, 4, 16 apply to Christendom?

become unclean. And you bring your days near, and you will come to your years. That is why I must make you an object of reproach to the nations and of jeering to all the lands. And you will certainly be profaned within yourself before the eyes of the nations, and you will have to know that I am Jehovah.' "—Ezekiel 22:3, 4, 16.

[12] Christendom's bloodguilty religion was cast off by the very God, Jehovah, whom she claims to worship, but whose name she no longer likes to use. In the year 1919 C.E., along with all Babylonian religion worldwide, she suffered a great fall. No longer could she have any standing before the Most High. No longer could she exercise control over true worshipers of Jehovah. Nor could any other part of Babylon the Great, the world empire of false religion. For "the Sovereign Lord Jehovah" now sounded forth this call to the faithful "holy ones" on earth:

" 'I, Jehovah, am your God, the One teaching you to benefit yourself, the One causing you to tread in the way in which you should walk.' Go forth, you people, out of Babylon! . . . Tell forth even with the sound of a joyful cry, cause this to be heard." (Isaiah 48:16, 17, 20)

What is this "sound of a joyful cry," and where has it been heard?

GLOBAL WITNESS GETS STARTED

[13] "The Son of man" described a prominent aspect of this "joyful cry" in his prophecy on "the conclusion of the system of things," saying:

"And this good news of the kingdom will be preached in

---

12. (a) What momentous event took place in 1919? (b) How did this benefit God's people on earth?
13. (a) What aspect of the "joyful cry" now became prominent? (b) What clarion call went forth?

***all the inhabited earth for a witness to all the nations; and then the end will come."* (*Matthew 24:3, 14, 37*)**

But the "holy ones" needed to be organized in order to get this work done. Nor could they accomplish it by mere human strength. Happily, at international conventions arranged at Cedar Point, Ohio, U.S.A., in 1919, and again in 1922, Jehovah's spirit was poured out upon them in a marvelous way. It organized and energized them to 'advertise, advertise, advertise the King and his kingdom.' (Matthew 24:31) For these "chosen ones" holding fast the heavenly hope, a grand work lay ahead.

[14] Just as Joel's prophecy had been fulfilled at Pentecost 33 C.E. during the "last days" of the Jewish system of things, now that prophecy began to have a major fulfillment during the "last days" of Satan's world system. Enlightened and motivated by God's spirit, modern-day anointed 'sons and daughters' of Jehovah did "certainly prophesy," as they got busy in warning the world of mankind of the approach of "the great and illustrious day of Jehovah," and of the urgent need to 'call on the name of Jehovah' in order to be saved.—Acts 2:16-21; Joel 2:28-32.

A FAITHFUL "SLAVE"

[15] In his great prophecy concerning the "sign," Jesus had asked a question:

"Who really is the faithful and discreet slave whom his master appointed over his domestics, to give them their food at the proper time?"

---

14. How did Joel's prophecy now have a major fulfillment?
15. (a) Who is the "faithful and discreet slave"? (b) How is it again identified in modern times?

THE KINGDOM THEME of the BIBLE

EDENIC PROMISE OF KINGDOM "SEED"

KINGLY "SEED" FORETOLD THROUGH ABRAHAM, DAVID

KINGDOM PREACHING— KING'S RANSOM SACRIFICE

1,000-YEAR KINGDOM
RESTORES PARADISE

KINGDOM 'COMES' TO
DESTROY MAN-RULE

KINGDOM ESTABLISHED
—"LAST DAYS" FROM 1914

A faithful "slave" class had served among the early Christians until the great apostasy set in. Do we again find such a "slave" organization dispensing spiritual food when the Lord Jesus comes into his kingdom? We do! Those "Bible Students," as they were then called, had done a global preparatory work. And Jesus said:

> ***"Happy is that slave if his master on arriving finds him doing so. Truly I say to you, He will appoint him over all his belongings."—Matthew 24:45-47.***

[16] Appreciating this appointment from the Master, the composite anointed "slave" has taken good care of Kingdom interests on earth, seeing to the publishing of the "good news." During the 1920's, powerful judgment messages were proclaimed against Satan and his organization, and especially against Babylonish religion. In 1931, the "slave" joyfully accepted the name that clearly set it apart from all false religion—the name "Jehovah's Witnesses" —along with the responsibility and privilege indicated by the prophet Isaiah in these words:

> ***" 'You are my witnesses,' is the utterance of Jehovah, 'even my servant whom I have chosen. . . . I—I am Jehovah, and besides me there is no savior. . . . You are my witnesses,' is the utterance of Jehovah, 'and I am God.' "—Isaiah 43:10-12.***

[17] How could the "slave," with the remaining anointed members numbering only in the tens of thousands, now get 'this good news of the kingdom preached in all the inhabited earth for a witness'? Jehovah was soon to supply the answer.

---

16. (a) How has the "slave" cared for the Master's "belongings"? (b) What Scriptural name has the "slave" joyfully accepted?
17. What question now called for an answer?

CHAPTER 16

"A GREAT CROWD" HAILS THE KING

THROUGH his prophet, Jehovah declared: "The little one himself will become a thousand, and the small one a mighty nation. I myself, Jehovah, shall speed it up in its own time." (Isaiah 60:22) And, wonderfully, Jehovah did proceed to "speed it up." In 1935 Jehovah's Witnesses assembled in convention at Washington, D.C., U.S.A. There it was made known that Jehovah was proceeding to gather "a great crowd" of "other sheep"—God-fearing persons who would, by the 'coming' of God's kingdom, gain everlasting life on a paradise earth.—John 10:16; Revelation 7:9.

[2] Revelation chapter 7 describes it thus: "After" the sealing of the "little flock" of Kingdom heirs, numbering 144,000, "a great crowd, which no man was able to number, out of all nations and tribes and peoples and tongues" is seen standing before God's throne. They acknowledge the sovereignty of Jehovah as exercised through his Christ. Joyfully they attribute salvation to God and to the Lamb. As a group, they will never need to die, for they are "the ones that come out of the great tribulation"

1, 2. (a) How did Jehovah proceed to fulfill his prophecy at Isaiah 60:22? (b) What remarkable revelation of divine truth was made in 1935?

to inherit everlasting life in the cleansed earth. —Revelation 7:4, 9, 10, 14; Luke 12:32.

[3] Have you taken your place among this "great crowd" of worshipers today? Are you one of the 2,000,000 and more of these that are 'rendering God sacred service' throughout the earth? True, you are surrounded still by Satan's wicked, oppressive world and may have to endure many pressures in your daily life. But if you are one of the Lord's "sheep," you are under God's protective care. You do not have to hunger or thirst anymore for lack of spiritual sustenance. No longer need you fear God's scorching displeasure, for the Lamb is shepherding you and guiding you to "fountains of waters of life." Thus, in a figurative way, you are already sharing in the fulfillment of the promise: "And God will wipe out every tear from their eyes."—Revelation 7:15-17.

THE KING BLESSES HIS "SHEEP"

[4] In Bible times, and even down to our day, an Oriental shepherd enjoyed a most intimate relationship with his sheep. He called each one by name, and they knew his voice and responded readily as he led them in and out of the sheepfold. In John chapter 10 Jesus drew on this in illustrating, first, the loving relationship between himself and his "little flock" of 144,000 anointed followers, saying: "I am the fine shepherd, and I know my sheep and my sheep know me, just as the Father knows me and I know the Father; and I surrender my soul in behalf of the sheep." These become part of

---

3. (a) Has the "little one" indeed become "a thousand"? (b) How may you share in the fulfillment of Revelation 7:15-17?
4. What is the relation of Jesus to his "little flock"?

"Abraham's seed," through which "all the families" of the earth are to bless themselves.—John 10:14, 15; Genesis 12:3; Galatians 3:28, 29.

[5] What, then, is the relation of "the fine shepherd" to the families of mankind that are to live forever on earth? A most blessed one! For Jesus says of these:

> ***"And I have other sheep, which are not of this fold [of the "little flock"]; those also I must bring, and they will listen to my voice, and they will become one flock, one shepherd."***

Today, a "great crowd" of these "other sheep" are to be observed as they pasture along with the "little flock"—all of them unitedly obeying the "voice" of their shepherd in preaching "this good news of the kingdom . . . in all the inhabited earth for a witness to all the nations." Happy is your portion if you are one of these! (John 10:16; Matthew 24:14) Under the Kingdom rule, the number of the "other sheep" will increase into the billions by means of the resurrection of the earthly dead, as God's purpose to populate the earth with righteous humans moves on to its completion.—Genesis 1:28.

[6] That the "other sheep" come into prominence at "the conclusion of the system of things" is shown by the illustration with which Jesus closes out his prophecy on the "sign" of his presence. (Matthew 24:3) He says:

> ***"When the Son of man arrives in his glory, and all the angels with him, then he will sit down on his glorious throne.***

---

5. (a) What further happy relationship is referred to at John 10:16? (b) What privileges do the "other sheep" enjoy now, and what is the future prospect for this group?
6. How does Jesus' prophecy indicate when the "other sheep" come into prominence?

And all the nations will be gathered before him, and he will separate people one from another, just as a shepherd separates the sheep from the goats. And he will put the sheep on his right hand, but the goats on his left." (*Matthew* 25:31-33)

Since the glorious King and his angels are invisible to human eyes, how does he carry out the separating work?

[7] The holy angels give direction to that work. (Revelation 14:6-12; compare Acts 8:26-29; 10:1-8.) And here on earth the remaining ones of the "little flock," who are called the King's "brothers" at Matthew 25:40, take the lead in the preaching of the "good news." The King judges people according to their response to his "brothers" and the Kingdom message that they proclaim. What they do to his "brothers" he counts as done to himself. People who receive the King's "brothers" hospitably are in line for a blessing. Are you one of these? Of course, you must follow through, in accepting the Kingdom message wholeheartedly and in becoming a dedicated, baptized servant of Jehovah, on the basis of Jesus' name—for "there is no salvation in anyone else."—Acts 4:12; Matthew 25:35-40.

[8] As one of the Lord's "other sheep," to what may you look forward? What will be the result of your obeying the "voice" of your "fine shepherd" and "king"? In pronouncing judgment, the King says to the humble "sheep" at his right hand of favor: "Come, you who have been blessed by my Father, inherit the kingdom prepared for you from the founding of the world." You may expect to

---

7. (a) How is the separating work directed? (b) What must you do to receive a favorable judgment, and why?
8. In what invitation and promises may you share?

share in these Kingdom blessings proceeding from our Father, as the 'righteous ones depart into everlasting life.' (Matthew 25:34, 46) Yes, you may expect to share in the fulfillment of many prophetic promises, such as that in Isaiah, which says of Jehovah: "He will actually swallow up death forever, and the Sovereign Lord Jehovah will certainly wipe the tears from all faces. And the reproach of his people he will take away from all the earth, for Jehovah himself has spoken it." Wicked men may reproach you only a short time longer. For God's promise is that all who hope in Jehovah will enter soon into a veritable "banquet" of good things in a "new earth." You want to share in that "banquet," do you not?—Isaiah 25:6-9; 66:22.

"GOATS" AND PERSECUTIONS

[9] It may not be easy for you to pursue a course of righteousness in these "last days." Satan and his dupes may ridicule you, as they make their last all-out attempt to ruin this earth and mankind on it. (2 Peter 3:3, 4; 2 Timothy 3:1) When you call on your neighbors with the Kingdom message, you may find some who display a goatlike disposition. This they do by showing indifference or rudeness, or by outright opposition.—Matthew 25:33, 42-45.

[10] However, as one of the Lord's "sheep" you should not try to judge who may be a "goat." It is for the King, not for his "sheep" here on earth, to do the judging. (Compare Romans 14:10-12.) And, though you may meet with opposition because of your becoming a proclaimer of the "good news," God will strengthen you to do his will, as the

9, 10. (a) Why is it not easy to pursue righteousness today? (b) What attitude should you take toward opposers, and what help may you expect from God?

apostle Peter indicated in these words: "The God of all undeserved kindness . . . will himself finish your training, he will make you firm, he will make you strong." (1 Peter 5:10; compare 2 Corinthians 12:10.) Also, the apostle Paul gives this fine admonition: "Do not loiter at your [Kingdom] business. Be aglow with the spirit. Slave for Jehovah. Rejoice in the hope. Endure under tribulation. Persevere in prayer."—Romans 12:11, 12.

[11] Your loyal service and fervent prayers to Jehovah, along with your exemplary Christian behavior, may result in some who at first *appeared* to be "goats" turning out to be "sheep." The patient, respectful conduct of Christian wives has often been effective in winning over unbelieving husbands "without a word." (1 Peter 3:1, 2) Certainly we do not want to see people "depart into everlasting cutting-off," but, rather, we should want to help them to shed goatish dispositions, so as to attain to everlasting life.—Matthew 25:41, 46.

LOYAL "SHEEP" KEEP INTEGRITY

[12] It is to be noted that the "sheep" of Jesus' illustration went out of their way to minister to the King's "brothers" while these were sick and in prison. And in some parts of the earth today, privation and persecution, sickness and imprisonment have been the experience not only of the "little flock" but also of the "other sheep" who are serving so loyally and unitedly with them. For example, during 1933 to 1945, when the Nazi Hit-

---

11. What may be the happy result of exemplary Christian behavior?
12. How have the King's "brothers" and the "sheep" supported one another in modern times?

ler was making his drive for world domination, Jehovah's Witnesses underwent bitter persecutions —first in the Nazi-Fascist countries and later in all the warring nations. Many, both of the "little flock" and of the Lord's "other sheep," were killed. But they conquered marvelously in holding fast their integrity to the King and his kingdom!

[13] The contrast between the compromising stand of Christendom's religions and the integrity of Jehovah's Witnesses under pressure has often been commented on by historians. For example, in the book *A History of Christianity*, published in London, England, in 1976, Paul Johnson says first of the Catholic and Evangelical churches in Hitler's Germany: "Both churches, in the main, gave massive support to the regime. The Catholic bishops welcomed 'the new, strong stress on authority in the German state'; Bishop Bornewasser told the Catholic youth in Trier Cathedral: 'With raised heads and firm step we have entered the new reich and we are prepared to serve it with all the might of our body and soul.' In January 1934, Hitler saw twelve Evangelical leaders, and after this meeting they . . . issued a communique which pledged 'the leaders of the German Evangelical Church unanimously affirm their unconditional loyalty to the Third Reich and its leader.' "

[14] Then, with reference to the few professing Christians who he said "stuck to their principles," the writer goes on to say: "The bravest were the Jehovah's Witnesses, who proclaimed their outright doctrinal opposition from the beginning and suffered accordingly. They refused any cooperation

---

13, 14. What contrast has been noted between the stand of Christendom's religions and that of Jehovah's Witnesses?

with the Nazi state which they denounced as totally evil. . . . Many were sentenced to death for refusing military service . . . ; or they ended in Dachau or lunatic asylums. A third were actually killed; ninety-seven per cent suffered persecution in one form or another. They were the only Christian group which aroused Himmler's admiration."

[15] Not as pacifists, but as Christian neutrals supporting the incoming kingdom of God, young Witnesses faced imprisonment and execution rather than break integrity, as testified to by a typical 'last letter' that appears herewith. Throughout the earth, whether in Axis or Allied countries, the King's "brothers" and their companion "sheep" were mobbed, beaten up, imprisoned and maltreated. But they conquered in their spiritual warfare. The Devil could not crack their loyalty to the Kingdom. Like Jesus before them, they proved themselves to be "no part" of Satan's world.—John 15:19.

THE KINGDOM'S EDUCATIONAL PROGRAM

[16] The Watch Tower Society's president, J. F. Rutherford, died in 1942, to be succeeded by Nathan H. Knorr. Shortly, Theocratic Ministry Schools were set up in all congregations of Jehovah's Witnesses, and these have served invaluably in training male and female Witnesses to speak the Kingdom message more effectively and persuasively to others. Over the years, various textbooks have been provided for these schools. Nor was the missionary field over-

---

15. (a) What is your reaction to the typical letter herewith? (b) What was Satan's effort during World War II, and what is the evidence that he failed?

16, 17. (a) What educational program and expanded work now opened up? (b) What fruitage of this work is to be noted?

NEUTRAL TO THE DEATH

During the second world war, many young witnesses of Jehovah paid for their neutrality with their lives. The following letter is typical of a number of 'last letters' that such courageous Witnesses wrote to their families. It was written by 23-year-old Marcel Sutter, of Alsace-Lorraine, a few hours before he was beheaded with an ax in Torgau prison, Germany, August 1942.

"My dearly beloved parents and sisters,

"When you receive this letter, I will no longer be alive. Only a few hours separate me from my death. I ask you to be strong and courageous; do not cry, for I have conquered. I have finished the course and kept the faith. May Jehovah God help me until the end. Only a short period of time separates us from the kingdom of our Lord Jesus Christ. Soon we will see each other again in a better world of peace and righteousness. I rejoice at the thought of that day, since then there will be no more sighing. How marvelous that will be! I am yearning for peace. During these last few hours I have been thinking of you and my heart is a little bitter at the thought of not being able to kiss you good-bye. But we must be patient. The time is near when Jehovah will vindicate his Name and prove to all creation that he is the only true God. I now wish to dedicate my last few hours to him, so I will close this letter and say good-bye until we meet again soon. Praise be to our God Jehovah! With my warm love and greetings,

"Your beloved son and brother,
Marcel"

looked. On February 1, 1943, the Watchtower Bible School of Gilead was established in New York State. From many countries of earth, thousands of experienced full-time ministers ("pioneers") have been brought to the U.S.A., trained and sent forth "into all the earth" to preach "this good news of the kingdom."—Matthew 24:14; Romans 10:18.

[17] What marvelous fruitage has resulted from this global campaign of education! As we move on in the

1980's, the total of persons partaking of the bread and the wine at the annual Memorial of Jesus' death, thus indicating their hope of being united with him in his heavenly kingdom, has dropped below 10,000, as more of the King's "brothers" finish their earthly course in integrity. But the total of other attenders, who have an interest in living forever on earth as subjects of the Kingdom, has risen above 5,700,000. In 43,000 and more congregations of Jehovah's Witnesses around the earth today, the "great crowd" of the "other sheep" are doing by far the greater part of the witness work. How grand your opportunity is to be one of these!

[18] Though their number dwindles, the anointed remnant of Jesus' "little flock," the "faithful and discreet slave" class, continues to oversee the Kingdom activity. (Matthew 24:45-47) To accomplish this, it works through a governing body, an arrangement similar to that in the first-century Christian congregation. (Acts 15:6; Luke 12:42-44) With the death of N. H. Knorr in 1977, Frederick W. Franz, at 83 years of age, became the fourth president of the Watch Tower Society. And on July 1, 1979, the *Watchtower* magazine itself became 100 years of age! Behind it is a century of Kingdom witnessing. Yes, by printed page and word of mouth, "this good news" of the established Kingdom has been proclaimed in all the earth for a witness. Are you one who is sharing in this privileged work after the pattern that Jesus left? As Paul admonished:

"Through him let us always offer to God a sacrifice of praise, that is, the fruit of lips which make public declaration to his name."—Hebrews 13:15.

---

18. (a) How has the "faithful and discreet slave" continued its service? (b) In what momentous work may you now share?

[19] The apostle Paul declared in another letter: "With the heart one exercises faith for righteousness, but with the mouth one makes public declaration for salvation." (Romans 10:10) Do you exercise faith in the "good news," which focuses now on the kingdom of God, established in the heavens since 1914? Are you 'making public declaration for salvation,' as you pray for God's kingdom to "come" with all of its destructive force to remove Satan's organization from the earth? Are you zealous in telling others 'publicly and from house to house' of the Kingdom blessings that will flow to all mankind when shortly God's will takes place, "as in heaven, also upon earth"? Are you loyally supporting the anointed "faithful and discreet slave" class of true Christians as they continue to take the lead in sounding forth the Kingdom message "into all the earth . . . , and to the extremities of the inhabited earth," and in 'making disciples of people of all the nations, baptizing and teaching them'?—Matthew 6:10; 24:14, 45-47; 28:19, 20; Acts 5:42; 20:20; Romans 10:18.

[20] You may enjoy a grand privilege today in thus 'rendering sacred service day and night before the throne of God.' At the same time you place yourself in line to be one of the "great crowd" that will inherit everlasting life on an earth made glorious. (Revelation 7:9-17) But first the Kingdom must "come" to fight Armageddon's war! What will Armageddon mean for mankind and our earth?

---

19. (a) What course did Paul encourage, involving "heart" and "mouth"? (b) What timely questions are here asked, and how do you respond?
20. What grand privilege may you now enjoy?

CHAPTER 17

THE KING FIGHTS AT ARMAGEDDON

AS WORLD War II drew to its close, U.S. General Douglas MacArthur said: "Men from the beginning of time have sought peace. . . . Military alliances, balances of power, leagues of nations, all in turn failed, leaving the only path to be by the crucible of war. The utter destructiveness of war now blocks out this alternative. We have had our last chance. If we will not devise some greater and more equitable system, our Armageddon will be at our door."

[2] Some 35 years later, how were the nations making out with regard to this "last chance"? The *Times* of London, England, had this to say under the headline "West Germans Fear Armageddon": "The spectre of war has returned to haunt West Germany as the international situation seems to be slipping inexorably out of control." And in an article entitled "World Stumbles into a Darkness," the editor of the Miami *Herald*, U.S.A., asked his readers whether it had dawned on them "that Armageddon isn't just some allegory that you read about in the Bible, it's real," and added: "Anyone with half a logical mind can put together the cataclysmic events of the past few years and see that

---

1, 2. What have people of the world been saying about Armageddon?

the world is at a historic threshold. . . . It will change forever the way men live."

[3] True, mankind stands at the threshold of great changes. But do we now face Armageddon? What is meant by Armageddon?

[4] Interestingly, Armageddon is different from what most people think. For the Bible describes the war at Armageddon, not as a cataclysmic war among earthly nations or blocs of nations, but as "the war of the great day of God the Almighty." It is *God's* war against "the kings of the entire inhabited earth"—meaning the rulers who refuse to submit when *God's* kingdom 'comes' to cause his will to be done on earth. (Psalm 2:6-12; Daniel 2:44) It is *God's* great act of destroying wicked nations and men, in preparing the way for Messiah's peaceful reign of 1,000 years.—Revelation 16:14, 16; Psalm 46:8, 9; 145:20; Joel 3:9-17; Nahum 1:7-9.

PRELIMINARIES TO THE BATTLE

[5] Revelation, chapters 16 to 18, tells us much about developments on earth just prior to the war at Armageddon. In the course of the prophecy, the invitation is extended: "Come, I will show you the judgment upon the great harlot who sits on many waters." This "great harlot" is later identified for us as "Babylon the Great, the mother of the harlots and of the disgusting things of the earth." Just as ancient Babylon, sitting astride the Euphrates River, became "mother" to the mystic system of religion that spread from Babylon throughout the earth, so "Babylon the Great" today is the world empire

---

3, 4. How does the Bible view of Armageddon differ?
5. How may we identify the "great harlot" of Revelation 17?

of false religion that holds spiritual dominion over "peoples and crowds and nations and tongues," to their hurt. (Revelation 17:1, 5, 15) It embraces the thousands of religious sects, great and small, "Christian" and non-Christian, that do not acknowledge and serve the true God, Jehovah.

[6] As a prelude to the war at Armageddon, we are shown an angel pouring out a bowl "of the anger of God." Where? "Upon the great river Euphrates, and its water was dried up, that the way might be prepared for the kings from the rising of the sun." (Revelation 16:1, 12) More than 600 years before the apostle John wrote down that prophecy, Kings Darius of Media and Cyrus of Persia invaded the land of Babylon from the east. Under cover of darkness, Cyrus diverted the Euphrates into other channels, and as the waters fell away he sent his army into the city by way of the riverbed. In one night, while Babylon's rulers and nobility were blaspheming Jehovah in a drunken orgy, that great city was overthrown.—Daniel 5:1-4, 30, 31.

[7] Do we see a modern-day parallel to this? Why, yes! The time has come for God to execute judgment on "Babylon the Great," and especially her "daughter" organizations of Christendom. Christendom's apostasy and bloodguilt have now come to the full! (Revelation 18:24; Jeremiah 51:12, 13) In recent times the "waters," or "peoples," that formerly supported her religion have been falling away. Support for religion has been drying up, with many persons turning to the teachings of Darwin, Marx,

---

6. Revelation 16 refers to what event that reminds of ancient Babylon?
7. What modern-day parallel do we now see?

Lenin and Mao. Also, as prophesied concerning the "last days," people have become "lovers of pleasures rather than lovers of God."—2 Timothy 3:1, 4.

[8] Contributing to the falling away of the "waters" has been the action of righteously inclined persons who have obeyed heaven's call with regard to "Babylon the Great":

"Get out of her, my people, if you do not want to share with her in her sins, and if you do not want to receive part of her plagues." (Revelation 18:4)

The world empire of false religion, and Christendom in particular, laments the closing of church buildings, the empty pews and the dwindling numbers of priests and nuns. However, those who now place themselves on the side of the Greater Darius, Jehovah God, and the Greater Cyrus, Christ Jesus, enter into a marvelous spiritual prosperity. Are you one of these?

PLAYING THE HARLOT

[9] "Babylon the Great," while professing to belong to God, has always had political connections, and in this sense 'the kings of the earth have committed fornication' with her. But now, in "the last days," she has her big opportunity! What is that? Ah, there comes to view "a scarlet-colored wild beast." What might this "beast" be? Without doubt it has reference to the political nations of earth, for these are

---

8. (a) What call have righteously inclined persons obeyed? (b) How does the state of false religion now contrast with that of true religion?

9, 10. (a) What fearsome "beast" appears in these "last days"? (b) In a public talk in 1942, how was it identified and its course described?

so often referred to in the Bible under the symbol of 'beasts.' (Revelation 13:1-4, 11-15; Daniel 7:3-8, 17-25; 8:5-8, 20-22) But here we have a combination "beast," for this fearsome animal has "seven heads and ten horns."—Revelation 17:3.

[10] What composite "beast" has appeared in these "last days," and what has been its performance on the world stage? At an international convention of Jehovah's Witnesses in 1942, the public talk entitled "Peace—Can It Last?" called attention to the prophecy at Revelation 17:7, 8. The speaker, Watch Tower president N. H. Knorr, identified "the wild beast that . . . was" as the League of Nations —brought forth in 1920. But now, in that wartime year of 1942, he stated: "The League is in effect in a state of suspended animation, and needs to be revived if it is ever to live again. It has gone into the abyss of inaction and ineffectiveness. It 'is not.'" President Knorr went on to show that "the wild beast that . . . was, but is not, . . . is about to ascend out of the abyss, and it is to go off into destruction." True to the Bible prophecy, that "beast" was revived in 1945 as the United Nations.

[11] This international "beast," brought forth to maintain "peace and security" among the nations, is in fact "full of blasphemous names," for it claims that it can do what only God's kingdom by Christ Jesus can accomplish. (Revelation 17:3) The apostle Paul prophesied of an occasion when the boastful rulers of Satan's world would be lauding themselves as peacemakers. He said:

"Jehovah's day is coming exactly as a thief in the night. Whenever it is that they are saying: 'Peace and security!' then

---

11. (a) Why is this "beast" described as being "full of blasphemous names"? (b) What judgment is in store for the "beast"?

***sudden destruction is to be instantly upon them just as the pang of distress upon a pregnant woman; and they will by no means escape."* (*1 Thessalonians 5:2, 3*)**

According to God's Word, the 'peace and security beast' will meet up with a quick, decisive execution of Jehovah's judgment!

"TOO BAD" FOR THE HARLOT!

[12] Despite God's declared disapproval of the blasphemous U.N. beast, "Babylon the Great" seeks to have amorous relations with it. Yes, she is pictured as sitting like a queen atop the "wild beast": "And the woman was arrayed in purple and scarlet, and was adorned with gold and precious stone and pearls and had in her hand a golden cup that was full of disgusting things and the unclean things of her fornication." Little marvel that John wrote of this situation: "Well, on catching sight of her I wondered with great wonderment"!—Revelation 17:4, 6.

[13] This liaison between the Babylonish world empire of false religion and the U.N. 'peace and security beast' turns out disastrously. Although the harlot-like "Babylon" may think that she sits pretty with that world body, God's Word foretells something else for her:

***"And the ten horns that you saw, and the wild beast, these will hate the harlot and will make her devastated and naked, and will eat up her fleshy parts and will completely burn her with fire."* (*Revelation 17:16*)**

---

12. What description of the "harlot" caused John to wonder?
13, 14. (a) What woeful end awaits false religion? (b) How will it come? (c) Who will mourn for Babylon the Great, but why from a distance?

A woeful end indeed for the world empire of false religion!

[14] The desolating of "Babylon the Great" will be swift.

"In one day her plagues will come, death and mourning and famine, and she will be completely burned with fire, because Jehovah God, who judged her, is strong." (Revelation 18:8)

But there will be those who mourn her. These will not be the militaristic "ten horns" that treacherously turn upon her, but others among the political rulers who used to hobnob with the clergy for the sake of appearances, and to help cover up their shady practices. These will lament over her from a distance, for fear they may share her fate, saying:

"Too bad, too bad, you great city, Babylon you strong city, because in one hour your judgment has arrived!"—Revelation 18:9, 10.

[15] There will also be men of Big Business, gangsters and other racketeers, who have used their religious connections to cast a veneer of "holiness" over their corrupt dealings and to soothe their guilty consciences. These, too, will take up the refrain:

"Too bad, too bad . . . , because in one hour such great riches have been devastated!" (Revelation 18:11-19)

The costly cathedrals, the accumulated lands and wealth, the huge bank accounts and commercial investments of the world's religion—all of these will have been laid waste.

[16] Hypocritical world religion, greedy commerce, corrupt politics—all three branches of Satan's orga-

---

15. Who else take up the refrain, and why?
16. What three groups are in line for execution?

THE "HARLOT" AND THE "BEAST"

What has been the relationship of the world empire of false religion with the 'peace and security beast'? Has "Babylon the Great" sought a controlling interest in the League of Nations and, later, the United Nations? Let the facts answer:

After the League of Nations was proposed in 1918, the "Bulletin" of the Federal Council of Churches of Christ in America went so far as to state: "As Christians we urge the establishment of a League of Free Nations at the coming Peace Conference. Such a League is not a mere political expedient; it is rather the political expression of the Kingdom of God on earth. . . . The heroic dead will have died in vain unless out of victory shall come a new earth wherein dwelleth righteousness."

On the occasion of the 20th birthday of the United Nations, in 1965, the Associated Press reported from San Francisco: "Seven international leaders of religious faiths with more than 2,000 million world-wide members joined prayerful hands under one roof today in support of the UN quest for world peace. Pope Paul VI sent his blessings from Rome . . . to the convocation for Catholics, Protestants, Jews, Hindus, Buddhists, Muslims and Eastern (Greek) Orthodox Christians. . . . Rabbi Louis Jacobs . . . described 'the UN as the sole hope for lasting peace in a world whose survival depends on it.' "

In October 1965, Pope Paul VI described the United Nations as "that greatest of all international organizations," and added: "The peoples of the earth turn to the United Nations as the last hope of concord and peace."

Addressing the U.N. General Assembly on October 2, 1979, Pope John Paul II said: "The formal reason for my intervention today is, without any question, the special bond of cooperation that links the apostolic see with the United Nations organization. . . . I hope that the United Nations will ever remain the supreme forum of peace and justice, the authentic seat of freedom of peoples and individuals in their longing for a better future." Yet not once in his 62-minute speech did the pope mention Jesus Christ or the Kingdom.

In embracing man-made substitutes in place of God's kingdom, false religion looks to a vain hope. After warning against trusting in human rulers, Psalm 146:3-6 tells us: "Happy is the one . . . whose hope is in Jehovah his God, the Maker of heaven and earth." And Luke 2:10-14 identifies mankind's Savior as "Christ the Lord."

nization on earth are in line for the execution of Jehovah's judgment. After false religion goes down, what next?

THE KING GOES INTO ACTION!

[17] Those radical political powers that devastate world religion have no eyes of spiritual understanding. They do not acknowledge the Messianic kingdom, established in 1914. Instead, they vigorously oppose those who proclaim that kingdom and who declare their Christian neutrality with regard to the politics and wars of worldly 'kingdoms.' —Revelation 12:17; John 17:14, 16.

[18] After disposing of "Babylon the Great," those beastly "horns" can be expected to make their final attack on the Christian witnesses of Jehovah, the apparently defenseless followers of the Lamb here on earth. (Ezekiel 38:14-16; Jeremiah 1:19) How will these foes make out in that warfare? The prophecy answers:

> ***"These will battle with the Lamb, but, because he is Lord of lords and King of kings, the Lamb will conquer them. Also, those called and chosen and faithful with him will do so." (Revelation 17:14)***

Though they take no part in that battle, the remaining ones of Jesus' anointed followers on earth, along with their companions who have also answered the call to "sacred service," will be preserved alive. Are you one of these who are praying even now for God's kingdom to "come" at Armageddon?—Romans 12:1, 2; compare 2 Chronicles 20:5, 6, 12-17.

17, 18. (a) What follows the desolating of "Babylon the Great," and why? (b) Who finally conquers? (c) Who will be preserved alive? (d) How may you be one of these?

[19] Yes, you may be an eyewitness and a survivor of that catastrophic war at Armageddon. You may be an observer as the "King of kings," accompanied by the angelic armies of heaven, fights in vindication of Jehovah's sovereignty. There you may see the climactic battle against wicked men, against proud nations and their mighty armies and the wealthy "merchants" that support them! Their multibillion-dollar nuclear arsenal will fail them in that warfare! Greedy profiteers, who have trafficked in oil and food supplies will find their ill-gotten gains valueless, as the world's stock markets collapse and the value of gold as a means of deliverance plummets to zero. For "this is what the Sovereign Lord Jehovah has said, 'A calamity, a unique calamity, look! it is coming. Into the streets they will throw their very silver, and an abhorrent thing their own gold will become. Neither their silver nor their gold will be able to deliver them in the day of Jehovah's fury. . . . and they will have to know that I am Jehovah.' "—Ezekiel 7:5, 19, 27.

[20] In that day of Armageddon, you may find security, not in any material possession, but in standing firmly on the side of Jehovah and his "King of kings." It will depend on your obedience to the prophet's words:

"Seek Jehovah, all you meek ones of the earth, who have practiced His own judicial decision. Seek righteousness, seek meekness. Probably you may be concealed in the day of Jehovah's anger." (Zephaniah 2:3; see also Isaiah 26:20, 21; Daniel 12:1.)

---

19. (a) Of what may you be an eyewitness and a survivor? (b) What valuable things will then fail?
20. Where may you find real security?

For at Armageddon, the King seated upon the symbolic white horse "judges and carries on war in righteousness." While he 'shepherds the nations with a rod of iron,' to their destruction, he will bring the white-robed "great crowd" out of the "great tribulation," shepherding them in love and 'guiding them to fountains of waters of life.' May you be one of these!—Revelation 19:11-16; 7:9, 14, 17.

[21] Alas for the U.N., its supportive governments and their amassed military might! Let them assemble at Armageddon "to wage the war with the one seated on the [white] horse and with his [heavenly] army"! All in vain! The "King of kings" hurls them, as it were, into a "fiery lake," to their destruction. The remnants of Satan's organization on earth are likewise liquidated, for the long sword of the King is powerful indeed, able to search out and destroy any enemy.—Revelation 19:17-21.

[22] By missiles and plagues dispatched from heaven, "Jehovah will scourge all the peoples" that fight in opposition to his kingdom, and, no doubt, in their confusion these will hurl their armaments of destruction against one another, for 'the hand of each one will actually come up against the hand of his companion.' But if you are one of those calling on the name of Jehovah, you "will get away safe."—Joel 2:31, 32; Zechariah 14:3, 12, 13; Ezekiel 38:21-23; Jeremiah 25:31-33.

[23] That will be the grand climax of Jesus' pro-

21. Who will assemble at Armageddon, but why in vain?
22. How do God's prophets describe the fight at Armageddon?
23. (a) Of what will this be the grand climax? (b) What words of Jesus should make us glad?

SEQUENCE OF EVENTS LEADING TO ARMAGEDDON

- Issue of world domination raised, nations multiply arms
- Drying up of people's support of world religion
- A notable cry of "Peace and security!" by the nations
- Militaristic "ten horns" of U.N. devastate world religion
- Beastly "horns" make final attack on 'Lamb's' followers
- "King of kings" destroys nations, armies at Armageddon

WITH SATAN AND DEMONS HURLED INTO ABYSS
CHRIST'S GLORIOUS MILLENNIAL REIGN BEGINS

phetic "sign"—"great tribulation such as has not occurred since the world's beginning until now, no, nor will occur again." How glad we can be that those days will be "cut short" for the sake of the "chosen ones"! You, too, may survive as one of the "sheep" whom Jesus invites to "inherit the kingdom"!—Matthew 24:21, 22; 25:33, 34.

[24] When the war at Armageddon is finished, Satan, the wicked instigator of man's misrule of the earth, will himself be seized, bound and hurled into the abyss "for a thousand years." Why so? It is "that he might not mislead the nations anymore." (Revelation 20:2, 3) Then will dawn the most glorious era in all human history. And what will the 1,000 years mean for those loyal ones who have worked and prayed for the 'coming' of the Kingdom? Doubtless, you will be interested to know.

---

24. (a) What action will then be taken against Satan, and why? (b) What follows?

CHAPTER 18

THE KINGDOM TRIUMPHANT!

WILL mankind be destroyed off this earth? No. And the Kingdom is the reason why. For it is the "King of kings and Lord of lords," the enthroned Jesus, who goes into action at the Kingdom's 'coming,' to crush Satan's earthly organization and its oppressive systems. At Armageddon, those would-be ruiners of the earth will themselves be brought to ruin.—Revelation 11:15, 18; 14:19, 20; 19:11-16.

2 Our God, Jehovah, has warned us to keep wide awake to what he is about to accomplish at Armageddon.

" 'Therefore keep yourselves in expectation of me,' is the utterance of Jehovah, 'till the day of my rising up to the booty, for my judicial decision is to gather nations, for me to collect together kingdoms, in order to pour out upon them my denunciation, all my burning anger; for by the fire of my zeal all the earth will be devoured.' "

But there will be survivors, many of them! And Jehovah is already preparing them, as described by these further words of the same prophecy:

---

1. (a) What is the reason for having confidence in mankind's future? (b) What will Armageddon mean for ruiners of the earth?
2, 3. (a) What warning does Zephaniah's prophecy sound? (b) What is required for survival?

"For then I shall give to peoples the change to a pure language, in order for them all to call upon the name of Jehovah, in order to serve him shoulder to shoulder."—Zephaniah 3:8, 9.

[3] Will you be one of those survivors? Yes, if you "call upon the name of Jehovah." How may you do this? By making the change to a "pure language" —taking into your heart the cleansing good news of God's kingdom, and acting upon it. (Mark 13:10) Exercising faith in God's provision through Christ, you must do as Peter admonished his own people 19 centuries ago: "Repent, therefore, and turn around so as to get your sins blotted out, that seasons of refreshing may come from the person of Jehovah." —Acts 3:19.

[4] Like Jesus, you must show yourself to be no part of Satan's world. (John 17:14, 16) By dedicating yourself to Jehovah through Christ and undergoing water baptism in symbol thereof, you may enter into a very intimate relationship with Jehovah God. (1 Peter 3:21) This intimacy you should seek always to cultivate, as you serve God "shoulder to shoulder" with all of his organized people on earth. According to your opportunity, you will want to share with these in making known "this good news of the kingdom" to all who will listen.—Matthew 24:14; Romans 10:10-18; Hebrews 13:15.

[5] Are you one who is thus responding to the "pure language" of Bible truth? Then place your implicit trust in Jehovah. "As a mighty One, he will save." —Zephaniah 3:17; Isaiah 12:2-5.

4, 5. (a) How may you come to enjoy intimacy with Jehovah? (b) How may you respond to the "pure language"?

[6] As you cultivate love for Jehovah and his righteousness, you also need to live in harmony with Bible principles. The apostle John gave this fine counsel:

> *"Do not be loving either the world or the things in the world. If anyone loves the world, the love of the Father is not in him; because everything in the world—the desire of the flesh and the desire of the eyes and the showy display of one's means of life—does not originate with the Father, but originates with the world. Furthermore, the world is passing away and so is its desire, but he that does the will of God remains forever." (1 John 2:15-17)*

"Forever"! Does that not make it worth while to do God's will zealously during the final days of Satan's wicked system? Does it not encourage us in these "last days" to keep close to Jehovah's organization, as represented on earth by the "faithful and discreet slave"?—Matthew 24:45-47.

A MONUMENTAL WORK

[7] As the smoke of Armageddon's battle clears, Jehovah's visible organization will still be here, ready for use in whatever way he directs. And may we be counted worthy, also, to be here individually! —Zephaniah 2:3; Psalm 25:8, 9, 20.

[8] God's people will need to keep organized under the Kingdom government in order to accomplish the monumental work of beautifying the cleansed earth, transforming our globe into a veritable "garden of God." (Compare Ezekiel 31:8.) Do you also

---

6. What fine counsel did John give, and what should this encourage us to do?
7. After Armageddon, what will remain?
8. (a) What will then be needed to accomplish God's work? (b) How will God's people have been prepared?

want to share in that work? A willing spirit and God-given energy will be needed to perform that task—the same kind of zeal that Jehovah's Witnesses now show in 'preaching this good news of the kingdom in all the earth.' All will need to be real workers after the example of the King, who said: "My Father has kept working until now, and I keep working."—John 5:17; 4:34.

[9] No doubt housing projects will flourish earth wide—not the constructing of ugly city blocks of tenements, but the landscaping of beautiful family residences in paradisaic surroundings. Yes, there will be much work to do, but it will be joyful, interesting work, a rewarding work concerning which King Solomon said, "There is nothing better" than that "every man should eat and indeed drink and see good for all his hard work."—Ecclesiastes 3:12, 13; compare Isaiah 65:17, 21-25.

[10] Under what conditions will the Lord's "other sheep" carry out their work? (John 10:16) Revelation chapter 21 tells us what we may expect. It describes "a new heaven and a new earth." No longer do corrupt human systems of government hold control in society, for "the former heaven and the former earth" have passed away. Also, the Devil and his subtle influence have been removed. No longer is there a confused "sea" of humanity, tossed to and fro as they pursue godlessness. Instead, a stable human society, the "new earth," will provide a firm basis for doing God's will. There you may follow out loyally the directives of

---

9. (a) What kind of work will there be? (b) What indicates this will be no drudgery?
10. What does Revelation 21:1-4 show as to conditions then?

the "new heaven," comprised of the King and his "bride" of 144,000 members. In its capacity as "the holy city, New Jerusalem," this royal "bride" will 'come down from heaven' in that it turns attention to the reconstruction work to be done on earth. And with what happy results! As John relates:

"Look! The tent of God is with mankind, and he will reside with them, and they will be his peoples. And God himself will be with them. And he will wipe out every tear from their eyes, and death will be no more, neither will mourning nor outcry nor pain be anymore. The former things have passed away."—Revelation 21:1-4.

[11] Notice that there is embodied in that promise the grand prospect that "death will be no more." It is expected that *millions* will find salvation through the "great tribulation" to enter into the blessings of the "new earth." (Revelation 7:9, 14) Yet thousands of millions, *billions,* will ultimately enjoy life here under the Kingdom. Why do we say "billions"? After the flood of Noah's day, Jehovah gave to the righteous survivors a mandate, saying: "Be fruitful and become many and fill the earth." This suggests the joyful prospect of human marriage and the bringing forth of children *in righteousness* for at least a time after Armageddon. (Genesis 9:1, 7; 10:1-32; Matthew 24:37) However, that will not be God's principal way of 'filling the earth' with mankind at that time. How, then, will God populate our globe, thus accomplishing his original purpose? (Genesis 1:28; Isaiah 45:18) It will be by repeating, billions of times over, his great miracle of the resurrection.

---

11. (a) What grand prospects await the millions of survivors? (b) How will God populate the earth?

"GOD . . . OF THE LIVING"

[12] On one occasion, Jesus answered his opposers, saying:

> ***"As regards the resurrection of the dead, did you not read what was spoken to you by God, saying, 'I am the God of Abraham and the God of Isaac and the God of Jacob'? He is the God, not of the dead, but of the living."***

From God's standpoint, those faithful men were as good as alive, and would be resurrected. The crowds were astounded at that teaching.—Matthew 22:31-33; Luke 20:37, 38.

[13] It is reasonable to expect that such faithful ones who endured persecution "that they might attain a better resurrection," along with integrity-keeping ones of the "other sheep" who today may die before Armageddon, would experience an early resurrection into the "new earth." Perhaps you yourself have lost dear ones in death, even faithful servants of God. What a joy to welcome these back from the dead, and to tell them of Jehovah's great act of vindication!—Hebrews 11:35.

[14] However, what of the others of mankind who have died down through almost 6,000 years of history? Jesus says: "Do not marvel at this, because the hour is coming in which *all* those in the memorial tombs will hear his voice and come out." (John 5:28, 29) "The dead, the great and the small," will come forth from the grave to stand before God's judgment throne.—Revelation 20:11-13.

---

12. What teaching of Jesus astounded the crowds?
13. What may be expected with regard to faithful "other sheep" who have died?
14. What marvelous hope is described at John 5:28, 29 and Revelation 20:11-13?

[15] Will that be a fearsome time for the resurrected ones? Religious pictures of the Last Judgment notwithstanding, it will be a most joyous time. For those resurrected ones will not be judged according to their wrong deeds of former times, but, rather,

15. Why will the judgment time not be fearsome?

according to their willingness to live up to the righteous requirements for life in the realm of God's kingdom. (Compare Romans 6:7.) And every effort will be made to help them along the pathway to complete reconciliation with God. The greatest educational program of all time will be carried forward under the Kingdom organization.

In the new earth, children brought forth in righteousness will experience none of the woes that plague families today

[16] "Scrolls" will be opened. These will be instructions published to help resurrected humans to perform those "deeds" that will qualify them for everlasting life. (Revelation 20:12) The educational facilities and programs in the "new earth," being directed by Jehovah and his Messianic King, will be far advanced in comparison with anything Satan's world has ever offered.

BLESSINGS FOR THE "GREAT CROWD"

[17] However, if you are one of the "great crowd" of Armageddon survivors, where will you fit into this picture? The apostle Paul said: "Just as in Adam all are dying, so also in the Christ all will be made alive." (1 Corinthians 15:22) You, too, will need the benefit of Christ's ransom, which he will use in raising mankind to perfection during his 1,000-year reign. You, too, will need to avail yourself of the education in the millennial "scrolls," in order loyally to perform the "deeds" that will lead to your name's being written in "the scroll of life."

[18] Today, your imperfect human brain is capable of absorbing and retaining only a fraction of its full potential. Perhaps you have been heard to exclaim, 'If only I could remember!' How thankful you should be for Christ's sacrifice! For, as part of the Kingdom's program for uplifting mankind not only will bodily aches and pains be removed but that marvelous creation—your human mind—will be perfected for studying out and retaining infor-

---

16. (a) What are the "scrolls"? (b) Why will education be far superior in the "new earth"?
17. On surviving into that "new earth," what will you need to do?
18. What Kingdom program should bring special joy?

mation, reasoning upon it and, above all, worshipfully appreciating the grand qualities of our God, Jehovah. Language barriers, which resulted from the confusion of tongues at the tower of Babel, will be removed, and all mankind will be taught one language so as to worship Jehovah together in unity, as suggested in Zephaniah 3:9.

[19] Perfect human hearts, also, will be motivated by love of God and neighbor. There is no wonder that the Sovereign Lord Jehovah addressed these words to his appreciative people:

"Here I am creating new heavens and a new earth; and the former things will not be called to mind, neither will they come up into the heart. But exult, you people, and be joyful forever in what I am creating. For here I am creating [New] Jerusalem a cause for joyfulness and her people a cause for exultation. And I will be joyful in Jerusalem and exult in my people; and no more will there be heard in her the sound of weeping or the sound of a plaintive cry." (Isaiah 65:17-19)

The radiant joy and exultation of the 144,000 co-rulers of Christ in his kingdom will be reflected to the billions of the Kingdom's subjects on earth as these advance toward human perfection.

JEHOVAH'S NAME FOREVER SANCTIFIED

[20] A thousand years will pass, just like one day from Jehovah's standpoint, and how brief a time it will seem also to humankind, so busily occupied in constructive works! (2 Peter 3:8) We can anticipate, too, that there will be relaxation time for happy associations and healthful exercise, the enjoyment

---

19. In what joy will the Kingdom's subjects share?
20. (a) Why will the 1,000 years pass quickly? (b) How did David bless Jehovah? (c) Are you moved to similar expressions of praise?

of music and other worthwhile arts, and always arrangements for worship of our Grand Creator. All will want to bless Jehovah, as did David in making arrangements for temple worship, saying:

"Yours, O Jehovah, are the greatness and the mightiness and the beauty and the excellency and the dignity; for everything in the heavens and in the earth is yours. Yours is the kingdom, O Jehovah, the One also lifting yourself up as head over all. The riches and the glory are on account of you, and you are dominating everything; and in your hand there are power and mightiness, and in your hand is ability to make great and to give strength to all. And now, O our God, we are thanking you and praising your beauteous name." —1 Chronicles 29:11-13.

[21] In harmony with this magnificent expression of praise, the One greater than David, Christ Jesus, will conclude his millennial reign of peace and reconstruction by doing what the apostle Paul foretold:

"Next, the end, when he hands over the kingdom to his God and Father, when he has brought to nothing all [opposing] government and all authority and power."

Once and for all, God-rule will have been shown to be the right kind of government, sufficiently powerful to bring everlasting benefits to worshipers of Jehovah. Under the Kingdom's benevolent rule, Adamic death will have been removed and all mankind made alive "in the Christ." Thus, the billions who then live on earth will have been "set free from enslavement to corruption and have the glorious freedom of the children of God."—Romans 8:21; 1 Corinthians 15:22-28.

---

21. (a) How will Christ conclude his millennial reign? (b) What will the Kingdom have accomplished?

[22] For a short season, Satan will be released from the abyss, to test the perfected world of mankind regarding its loyalty to Jehovah's kingship. An indefinite number may choose to follow the Devil, but judgment will be executed swiftly upon them. The "seed" of God's "woman," Christ Jesus, will perform his final act of vindication by crushing the head of the original Serpent, annihilating him and his brood as completely as by fire that lasts "day and night forever and ever." The great issue raised in Eden as to Jehovah's rightful sovereignty over his creatures will have been tried and settled for all time!—Revelation 20:7-10; Genesis 3:15.

[23] When we reflect on the marvelous promises of the "King of eternity," our Grand Creator, the Sovereign Lord Jehovah, are we not moved in thankfulness to praise his name? Are we not moved, as were some on the day of Pentecost, to speak about "the magnificent things of God," about his "King of kings" and the Messianic Kingdom? (Acts 2:11; Revelation 15:3; 19:16) Are we not moved to pray to our heavenly Father, "LET YOUR KINGDOM COME"? (Matthew 6:9, 10) Yes, "COME," to destroy Satan's works and organization out of the earth! Yes, "COME," to provide for all mankind the right kind of government! Yes, "COME," to bring in the glorious millennial reign for the restoration of paradise, the resurrecting of the dead and the uplifting of all willing mankind to human perfection! Yes, "COME," that Jehovah's matchless name may be sanctified for all eternity!

---

22. (a) What short season of testing will follow? (b) What final act of vindication will Jesus perform?
23. (a) Reflection on God's promises should cause us to do what? (b) Why should we want to see 'God's kingdom come'?

APPENDIX TO CHAPTER 14

Historians hold that Babylon fell to Cyrus' army in October 539 B.C.E. Nabonidus was then king, but his son Belshazzar was coruler of Babylon. Some scholars have worked out a list of the Neo-Babylonian kings and the length of their reigns, from the last year of Nabonidus back to Nebuchadnezzar's father Nabopolassar.

According to that Neo-Babylonian chronology, Crown-prince Nebuchadnezzar defeated the Egyptians at the battle of Carchemish in 605 B.C.E. (Jeremiah 46:1, 2) After Nabopolassar died Nebuchadnezzar returned to Babylon to assume the throne. His first regnal year began the following spring (604 B.C.E.).

The Bible reports that the Babylonians under Nebuchadnezzar destroyed Jerusalem in his 18th *regnal* year (19th when accession year is included). (Jeremiah 52:5, 12, 13, 29) Thus if one accepted the above Neo-Babylonian chronology, the desolation of Jerusalem would have been in the year 587/6 B.C.E. But on what is this secular chronology based and how does it compare with the chronology of the Bible?

Some major lines of evidence for this secular chronology are:

Ptolemy's Canon: Claudius Ptolemy was a Greek astronomer who lived in the second century C.E. His Canon, or list of kings, was connected with a work on astronomy that he produced. Most modern historians accept Ptolemy's information about the Neo-Babylonian kings and the length of their reigns (though Ptolemy does omit the reign of Labashi-Marduk). Evidently Ptolemy based his historical information on sources dating from the Seleucid period, which began more than 250 years after Cyrus captured Babylon. It thus is not surprising that Ptolemy's figures agree with those of Berossus, a Babylonian priest of the Seleucid period.

Nabonidus Harran Stele (*NABON H 1, B*): This contemporary stele, or pillar with an inscription, was discovered in 1956. It mentions the reigns of the Neo-Babylonian kings Nebuchadnezzar, Evil-Merodach, Neriglissar. The figures given for these three agree with those from Ptolemy's Canon.

VAT 4956: This is a cuneiform tablet that provides astronomical information datable to 568 B.C.E. It says that the observations were from Nebuchadnezzar's 37th year. This would correspond to the chronology that places his 18th regnal year in 587/6 B.C.E. However, this tablet is admittedly a copy made in the third century B.C.E. so it is possible that its historical information is simply that which was accepted in the Seleucid period.

Business tablets: Thousands of contemporary Neo-Babylonian cuneiform tablets have been found that record simple business transactions, stating the year of the Babylonian king when the transaction occurred. Tablets of this sort have been found for all the years of reign for the known Neo-Babylonian kings in the accepted chronology of the period.

From a secular viewpoint, such lines of evidence might seem to establish the Neo-Babylonian chronology with Nebuchadnezzar's 18th year (and the destruction of Jerusalem) in 587/6 B.C.E. However, no historian can deny the possibility that the present picture of Babylonian history might be misleading or in error. It is known, for example, that ancient priests and kings sometimes altered records for their own purposes. Or, even if the discovered evidence is accurate, it might be misinterpreted by modern scholars or be incomplete so that yet undiscovered material could drastically alter the chronology of the period.

Evidently realizing such facts, Professor Edward F. Campbell, Jr., introduced a chart, which included Neo-Babylonian chronology, with the caution: "It goes without saying that these lists are provisional. The more one studies the intricacies of the chronological problems in the ancient Near East, the less he is inclined to think of any presentation as final. For this reason, the term *circa* [about] could be used even more liberally than it is."—*The Bible and the Ancient Near East* (1965 ed.), p. 281.

Christians who believe the Bible have time and again found that its words stand the test of much criticism and have been proved accurate and reliable. They recognize that as the inspired Word of God it can be used as a measuring rod in evaluating secular history and views. (2 Timothy 3:16, 17) For instance, though the Bible spoke of Belshazzar as ruler of Babylon, for centuries scholars were confused about him because no secular documents were available as to his existence, identity or position. Finally, however, archaeologists discovered secular records that confirmed the Bible. Yes, the Bible's internal harmony and the care exercised by its writers, even in matters of chronology, recommends it so strongly to the Christian that he places its authority above that of the ever-changing opinions of secular historians.

But how does the Bible help us to determine when Jerusalem was destroyed, and how does this compare to secular chronology?

The prophet Jeremiah predicted that the Babylonians would destroy Jerusalem and make the city and land a desolation. (Jeremiah 25:8, 9) He added: "And all this land must become a devastated place, an object of astonishment, and these nations will have to serve the king of Babylon seventy years." (Jeremiah 25:11) The 70 years expired when Cyrus the Great, in his first year, released the Jews and they returned to their homeland. (2 Chronicles 36:17-23) We believe that the most direct reading of Jeremiah 25:11 and other texts is that the 70 years would date from when the Babylonians destroyed Jerusalem and left the land of Judah desolate.—Jeremiah 52:12-15, 24-27; 36:29-31.

Yet those who rely primarily on secular information for the chronology of that period realize that if Jerusalem were destroyed in 587/6 B.C.E. certainly it was not 70 years until Babylon was conquered and Cyrus let the Jews return to their homeland. In an attempt to harmonize matters, they claim that Jeremiah's prophecy began to be fulfilled in 605 B.C.E. Later writers quote Berossus as saying that after the battle of Carchemish Nebuchadnezzar extended Babylonian influence into all Syria-Palestine and, when returning to Babylon (in his accession year, 605 B.C.E.), he took Jewish captives into exile. Thus they figure the 70 years as a period of servitude to Babylon beginning in 605 B.C.E. That would mean that the 70-year period would expire in 535 B.C.E.

But there are a number of major problems with this interpretation:

Though Berossus claims that Nebuchadnezzar took Jewish captives in his accession year, there are no cuneiform documents supporting this. More significantly, Jeremiah 52:28-30 carefully reports that Nebuchadnezzar took Jews captive in his seventh year, his 18th year and his 23rd year, *not* his accession year. Also, Jewish historian Josephus states that in the year of the battle of Carchemish Nebuchadnezzar conquered all of Syria-Palestine "excepting Judea," thus contradicting Berossus and conflicting with the claim that 70 years of Jewish servitude began in Nebuchadnezzar's accession year.—*Antiquities of the Jews* X, vi, 1.

Furthermore, Josephus elsewhere describes the destruction of Jerusalem by the Babylonians and then says that "all Judea and Jerusalem, and the temple, continued to be a desert for seventy years." (*Antiquities of the Jews* X, ix, 7) He pointedly states that "our city was *desolate* during the interval of seventy years, until the days of Cyrus." (*Against Apion* I, 19) This agrees with 2 Chronicles 36:21 and Daniel 9:2 that the foretold 70 years were 70 years of full desolation for the land. Second-century (C.E.) writer Theophilus of Antioch also shows that the 70 years commenced with the destruction of the temple after Zedekiah had reigned 11 years.—See also 2 Kings 24:18–25:21.

But the Bible itself provides even more telling evidence against the claim that the 70 years began in 605 B.C.E. and that Jerusalem was destroyed in 587/6 B.C.E. As mentioned, if we were to count from 605 B.C.E., the 70 years would reach down to 535 B.C.E. However, the inspired Bible writer Ezra reported that the 70 years ran until "the first year of Cyrus the king of Persia," who issued a decree allowing the Jews to return to their homeland. (Ezra 1:1-4; 2 Chronicles 36:21-23) Historians accept that Cyrus conquered Babylon in October 539 B.C.E. and that Cyrus' first regnal year began in the spring of 538 B.C.E. If Cyrus' decree came late in his first regnal year, the Jews could easily be back in their homeland by the seventh month (Tishri) as Ezra 3:1 says; this would be October 537 B.C.E.

However, there is *no reasonable way* of stretching Cyrus' first year from 538 down to 535 B.C.E. Some who have tried to explain away the problem have in a strained manner claimed that in speaking of "the first year of Cyrus" Ezra and Daniel were using some peculiar *Jewish* viewpoint that differed from the official count of Cyrus' reign. But that cannot be sustained, for both a non-Jewish governor and a document from the Persian archives agree that the decree occurred in Cyrus' first year, even as the Bible writers carefully and specifically reported.—Ezra 5:6, 13; 6:1-3; Daniel 1:21; 9:1-3.

Jehovah's "good word" is bound up with the foretold 70-year period, for God said:

"This is what Jehovah has said, 'In accord with the fulfilling of seventy years at Babylon I shall turn my attention to you people, and I will establish toward you my good word in bringing you back to this place.' " (Jeremiah 29:10)

Daniel relied on that word, trusting that the 70 years were not a 'round number' but an exact figure that could be counted on. (Daniel 9:1, 2) And that proved to be so.

Similarly, we are willing to be guided primarily by God's Word rather than by a chronology that is based principally on secular evidence or that disagrees with the Scriptures. It seems evident that the easiest and most direct understanding of the various Biblical statements is that the 70 years began with the complete desolation of Judah after Jerusalem was destroyed. (Jeremiah 25:8-11; 2 Chronicles 36:20-23; Daniel 9:2) Hence, counting back 70 years from when the Jews returned to their homeland in 537 B.C.E., we arrive at 607 B.C.E. for the date when Nebuchadnezzar, in his 18th regnal year, destroyed Jerusalem, removed Zedekiah from the throne and brought to an end the Judean line of kings on a throne in earthly Jerusalem.—Ezekiel 21:19-27.

The 'coming' of God's kingdom will mean more for mankind than any other event in history. That is why all of us need to be fully informed concerning the Kingdom.

Jehovah's Witnesses will be happy to discuss this vital topic with you, free of charge, on a family or an individual basis. Just write to the address for your country, as listed on the last page of this book, requesting such a Bible discussion. Arrangements will be made for a qualified Witness to call on you and help you to come to a clear understanding of the Kingdom, using, for example, the Questions for Discussion in this book.

Millions of persons in all parts of the earth have already been benefitted by this free service. You, too, may obtain the satisfying answers that will help you to build faith in God's kingdom.

Would you like to read God's Word in easy-to-understand, accurately translated English? More than 48,000,000 copies of the "New World Translation of the Holy Scriptures" have already been printed. You may request your copy of the latest edition of this valuable Bible, sending a contribution of $3.50 (U.S.) toward the printing cost to the appropriate address on page 192.

(Contribution subject to change)

REJOICE AT THE "GOOD NEWS"!

HERE are four books, the same size as the one you now hold in your hand, that will further enlighten you concerning the grandest good news ever proclaimed to humans:

TRUE PEACE AND SECURITY—HOW CAN YOU FIND IT?—This book points to the lasting solution to problems that press in on people everywhere. It reveals how true peace and security soon will be realized earth wide and what you must do now to benefit.

SURVIVAL INTO A NEW EARTH—A book that shows you how to survive the troubles ahead. It answers such questions as: What are you facing that is more awesome than a nuclear war? Is there a way around it? When is it expected? Are you marked for survival?

HAPPINESS—HOW TO FIND IT—A book showing that it really makes sense to believe in God, even in a world that has been influenced greatly by atheistic, evolutionist theories. It shows how to cope with life's problems now, while preparing for a happy future.

MAKING YOUR FAMILY LIFE HAPPY—A splendid aid for finding the key to family happiness. Discussed herein is every aspect of marriage, laying a fine foundation for it, the roles of husband and wife, the rearing of children and building as a family for life everlasting.

Any one of the above books is available for a contribution of $1 (U.S.). All four for just $4 (U.S.).

(Contributions subject to change)

Order from the nearest address listed on the next page.

CHIEF OFFICE AND OFFICIAL ADDRESS OF
Watch Tower Bible and Tract Society of Pennsylvania
Watchtower Bible and Tract Society of New York, Inc.
International Bible Students Association
25 Columbia Heights, Brooklyn, New York 11201, U.S.A.

ADDRESSES OF BRANCH OFFICES:

ALASKA 99507: 2552 East 48th Ave., Anchorage. **ARGENTINA:** Caldas 1551, 1427 Buenos Aires. **AUSTRALIA:** Box 280, Ingleburn, N.S.W. 2565; Zouch Road, Denham Court, N.S.W. 2565. **AUSTRIA:** Gallgasse 42-44, Postfach 67, A-1134 Vienna. **BAHAMAS:** Box N-1247, Nassau, N.P. **BARBADOS:** Fontabelle Rd., Bridgetown. **BELGIUM:** rue d'Argile 60, B-1950 Kraainem. **BELIZE:** Box 257, Belize City. **BOLIVIA:** Casilla No. 1440, La Paz. **BRAZIL:** Rodovia SP-141, Km 43, 18280 Cesario Lange, SP; Caixa Postal 92, 18270 Tatuí, SP. **BURMA:** P.O. Box 62, Rangoon. **CANADA L7G 4Y4:** Box 4100, Halton Hills (Georgetown), Ontario. **CHILE:** Av. Concha y Toro 3456, Puente Alto; Casilla 267, Puente Alto. **COLOMBIA:** Apartado Aereo 85058, Bogotá 8, D.E. **COSTA RICA:** Apartado 10043, San José. **COTE D'IVOIRE (IVORY COAST):** 06 B.P. 393, Abidjan 06. **CYPRUS:** P. O. Box 4091, Limassol. **DENMARK:** P.B. 340; Stenhusvej 28, DK-4300 Holbæk. **DOMINICAN REPUBLIC:** Avenida Francia 33 (Apartado 1742), Santo Domingo. **ECUADOR:** Casilla 4512, Guayaquil. **EL SALVADOR:** Apartado 401, San Salvador. **ENGLAND NW7 1RN:** The Ridgeway, London. **FIJI:** Box 23, Suva. **FINLAND:** Postbox 68, SF-01301 Vantaa 30. **FRANCE:** 81 rue du Point-du-Jour, F-92100 Boulogne-Billancourt. **GERMANY, FEDERAL REPUBLIC OF:** Postfach 20, D-6251 Selters/Taunus 1. **GHANA:** Box 760, Accra. **GREECE:** 77 Leoforos Kifisias, GR-151 24 Marousi. **GUADELOUPE:** B.P. 239, 97156 Pointe-à-Pitre Cedex. **GUAM 96913:** 143 Jehovah St., Barrigada. **GUATEMALA:** 11 Avenida 5-67, Guatemala 1. **GUYANA:** 50 Brickdam, Georgetown 16. **HAITI:** Post Box 185, Port-au-Prince. **HAWAII 96819:** 2055 Kam IV Rd., Honolulu. **HONDURAS:** Apartado 147, Tegucigalpa. **HONG KONG:** 4 Kent Road, Kowloon Tong. **ICELAND:** P. O. Box 8496, IS-128 Reykjavík. **INDIA:** Post Bag 10, Lonavla, Pune Dis., Mah. 410 401. **IRELAND:** 29A Jamestown Road, Finglas, Dublin 11. **ISRAEL:** P. O. Box 961, 61-009 Tel Aviv. **ITALY:** Via della Bufalotta 1281, I-00138 Rome RM. **JAMAICA:** Box 180, Kingston 10. **JAPAN:** 1271 Nakashinden, Ebina City, Kanagawa Pref., 243-04. **KENYA:** Box 47788, Nairobi. **KOREA, REPUBLIC OF:** Box 33 Pyungtaek P. O., Kyunggido, 180. **LEEWARD ISLANDS:** Box 119, St. Johns, Antigua. **LIBERIA:** P.O. Box 171, Monrovia. **LUXEMBOURG:** 41, rue du Père Raphaël, L-2413 Luxembourg, G. D. **MADAGASCAR:** B.P. 511, Antananarivo 101. **MALAYSIA:** 28 Jalan Kampar, Off Jalan Landasan, 41300 Klang, Sel. **MARTINIQUE:** Cours Campeche, Morne Tartenson, 97200 Fort de France. **MAURITIUS:** 5 Osman Ave., Vacoas. **MEXICO:** Apartado Postal 42-048, 06471 México, D.F. **NETHERLANDS:** Noordbargerstraat 77, 7812 AA Emmen. **NETHERLANDS ANTILLES:** Oosterbeekstraat 11, Willemstad, Curaçao. **NEW CALEDONIA:** B.P. 787, Nouméa. **NEW ZEALAND:** P.O. Box 142; 198 Mahia Rd., Manurewa. **NIGERIA:** PMB 001, Shomolu, Lagos State. **NORWAY:** Gaupeveien 24, N-1914 Ytre Enebakk. **PAKISTAN:** 197-A Ahmad Block, New Garden Town, Lahore 16. **PANAMA:** Apartado 1835, Panama 9A. **PAPUA NEW GUINEA:** Box 636, Boroko, N.C.D. **PERU:** Av. El Cortijo 329, Monterrico Chico, Lima 33; Casilla 18-1055, Miraflores, Lima 18. **PHILIPPINES, REPUBLIC OF:** P.O. Box 2044, Manila 2800; 186 Roosevelt Ave., San Francisco del Monte, Quezon City 3010. **PORTUGAL:** Av. D. Nuno Álvares Pereira, 11, P-2765 Estoril. **PUERTO RICO 00927:** Calle Onix 23, Urb. Bucaré, Río Piedras. **SENEGAL:** B.P. 3107, Dakar. **SIERRA LEONE:** P. O. Box 136, Freetown. **SOLOMON ISLANDS:** P.O. Box 166, Honiara. **SOUTH AFRICA:** Private Bag 2067, Krugersdorp, 1740. **SPAIN:** Apartado postal 132, E-28850 Torrejón de Ardoz (Madrid). **SRI LANKA, REP. OF:** 62 Layard's Road, Colombo 5. **SURINAME:** Wicherstraat 8-10; Box 49, Paramaribo. **SWEDEN:** Box 5, S-732 00 Arboga. **SWITZERLAND:** Ulmenweg 45; P.O. Box 225, CH-3602 Thun. **TAHITI:** B.P. 518, Papeete. **TAIWAN:** 109 Yun Ho Street, Taipei 10613. **THAILAND:** 69/1 Soi 2, Sukhumwit Rd., Bangkok 10 110. **TRINIDAD:** Lower Rapsey Street & Laxmi Lane, Curepe. **UNITED STATES OF AMERICA:** 25 Columbia Heights, Brooklyn, N.Y. 11201. **URUGUAY:** Francisco Bauzá 3372, Montevideo. **VENEZUELA:** Apartado 116, La Victoria, Edo. Aragua 2121A. **WESTERN SAMOA:** P. O. Box 673, Apia. **ZAMBIA, REP. OF:** Box 21598, Kitwe. **ZIMBABWE:** 35 Fife Avenue, Harare.